the long and winding road

the long and winding road

DISCOVERING THE PLEASURES
AND TREASURES OF **HIGHWAY 97**

Jim Couper

VANCOUVER · VICTORIA · CALGARY

Heritage House Publishing Company Ltd.
#108–17665 66A Avenue, Surrey, BC V3S 2A7
www.heritagehouse.ca

Library and Archives Canada Cataloguing in Publication

Couper, Jim

The long and winding road: discovering the pleasures and treasures of Highway 97 / Jim Couper.

Includes index.
ISBN-13: 978-1-894974-12-7
ISBN-10: 1-894974-12-3

1. United States Highway 97—History. 2. Highway 97 (B.C.)—History. 3. Pacific States—Description and travel. 4. British Columbia—Description and travel. 5. Automobile travel—Pacific States—Guidebooks. 6. Automobile travel—British Columbia—Guidebooks. I. Title.

F851.C685 2006   917.9   C2006-903117-7

Edited by Margaret Tessman
Book design and layout by Jacqui Thomas
Maps by Darlene Nickull except for page 15, by Ana Tercero
All photos by Jim Couper
Printed in Canada

Heritage House acknowledges the financial support for its publishing program from the Government of Canada through the Book Publishing Industry Development Program (BPIDP), Canada Council for the Arts, and the British Columbia Arts Council.

BRITISH COLUMBIA
ARTS COUNCIL
Supported by the Province of British Columbia

DEDICATION

To my wife, Lian, who never tires of back lanes and country roads; to our children, Dylan and Sara-Jill, who treat Africa and India as casually as one treats a backyard; and to my parents, Florence and Archie, who instilled my joy of travel with weekends in northern Ontario and wonderful family vacactions to their homeland, Scotland.

ACKNOWLEDGEMENTS

Thanks to KOA campgrounds for allowing me the use of their facilities. The chambers of commerce and/or visitor and convention bureaus of the following cities helped greatly in introducing me to the local sights: Bend, Clearwater Lake, Dawson Creek, Dorris, Fort St. John, Kamloops, Klamath Falls, Lac La Hache, Osoyoos, Penticton, Prince George, Weed, Wenatchee, Williams Lake and Yakima.

Contents

The Road Ahead

WHEN I MOVED TO BRITISH COLUMBIA'S OKANAGAN VALLEY IN 1996, THE FIRST road I became familiar with was Highway 97—it was the backbone of the valley. Exploring my new home territory, I sensed that I was not on a mundane, everyday road, but was riding atop something with extraordinary character.

As I gained familiarity with my new surroundings it was always a pleasure to drive this road that hugged the shorelines of seven different local lakes while good-naturedly following both hill and dale. I frequently drove to Kamloops, and while writing my first tour guide, *Discovering the Okanagan*, I went as far south as the Columbia River in Washington State. I'm embarrassed to admit that it was not until I was almost finished compiling that book that I got to wondering where 97 originated and where it went.

I got out my British Columbia road map and found that 97 went right off the bottom edge. Following the red line south, I had to unfold a Washington map all the way to Oregon, and when I opened the Oregon map I realized that the blacktop continued into California. The map of that big western state showed that my favourite road ended in the town of Weed, just south of the Oregon border. As my finger travelled north, it traced 97 all the way to the Yukon border.

The mapping program on my computer determined the length of 97 to be 3,290 kilometres (2,044 miles). Clearly, it was the longest road in British Columbia, if not on the continent (the Trans-Canada

Highway, which connects the Pacific to the Atlantic, had that undisputed title). But could 97 be the longest north-south route? Interstate Highway 75 in the east—from the tip of Florida to the top of Michigan —looked like a contender, although when I plotted the distance, it fell short by 480 kilometres (300 miles). Then I noticed that I-95 runs from Miami to the top of Maine. Closer, but still 160 kilometres (100 miles) short.

Route 66, a legend that has outlived its glory days, runs diagonally from Chicago to San Diego and it's longer than 97 by a few hundred miles. But, being diagonal, it didn't make the grade as a north-south route. Additionally, it is a decommissioned road that doesn't really exist anymore except in a Nat King Cole song and in reruns of a TV show. Grab a modern road map and you won't even find Route 66.

The only serious contender that remained was Highway 1 in the eastern United States, which meanders from Key West, Florida, to the corner of Maine. Counting every little twist and turn, it clearly out-distances Highway 97. Alas, it shares a similar problem to Route 66—sections of it simply disappear. While Highway 1 is a worthy and interesting route, it didn't meet my criteria, as it is not continuous.

I have sheepishly admitted that, despite residing a few kilometres from it, I had never questioned the origin or destination (interchangeable terms when speaking of a road) of Highway 97. Apparently my ignorance is shared by millions of others, including many who work in the tourist trade and should know a thing or two about a major artery. It's rare to meet anyone who is actually aware of the extent of 97. One exception is the people in the town of Weed, California, which touts itself as the start of both 97 and the "Alcan Highway." Bravo!

Before getting into the details of 97 I should expose my biases so you can make allowances for my prejudices. I like small towns and downtowns. I detest the mega-mart commercial strips, and fast food restaurants are not my idea of dining in style. When I get close to these places I have to check the licence plates to know if I am in Kansas, California or Saskatchewan. They all appear to be cut from the same corporate cloth.

I like downtowns because you can walk through them, meet local people, sit on a bench under a tree, and have a unique experience. There is no better place to people-watch, and each person has an interesting story to tell. Downtown shops are generally locally owned, reflecting independent thought. For me, the reason for touring is to get off the beaten track and do things that are a little different. So I'll go into Java Joe's Downtown Dive and, whether the coffee is great or terrible, I'll have something to remember.

Of the events that take place in the villages and cities along Highway 97, my selections are based on two criteria. First, the various celebrations must have passed the test of time and have run for at least five successive years. Additionally, they must be major events that attract people from the surrounding area and they also must have some relationship to nostalgia, gold mining, history, culture, geology or ecology. You will not find triathlons, wakeboard competitions, motorcycle races or downhill ski events listed, but you will find quilt-making festivals, gold-panning jamborees, apple expositions and fall fairs.

Two major festivities are intentionally missing from the listings: July 1 and July 4. We can assume that Canada Day and Independence Day will be celebrated, to different degrees, by every town and city along Highway 97. To avoid repetition, these events are omitted.

Starting Out

Our journey starts at the sleepy northern California town of Weed, 320 kilometres (200 miles) by road from the Pacific Ocean and 92 kilometres (53 miles) south of the California–Oregon border.

Wandering northward, 97 connects, like a child's dot-to-dot, a multitude of small towns and medium-sized cities. The California section travels through beautiful arid uplands where lakes and rivers are often in view. Old-fashioned motels, cabins and lodges reach out like lights at the end of a time tunnel taking us back to the 1960s, or even the 1930s.

Like a lazy slithering serpent, nostalgic 97 wanders northward through the dry interior of Oregon and Washington and bridges the mighty Columbia River three times. It then traverses the dusty Okanogan (two Os and two As) and crosses, with little fanfare, the international border at the 49th parallel and becomes an essential part of British Columbia. North of 49, the landscape is suddenly rich with irrigated orchards and vineyards and the houses and cars exude a sense of affluence. The Canadian Okanagan (one O and three As) is the most developed and populated area that 97 passes through. The long gentle lake, warm temperatures and sunny summer skies are magnets for vacationers and retirees. Here, the fur trade and ranching, rather than gold, were responsible for the first roads.

Past the Okanagan, 97 enters the Thompson Plateau region and forks northwest to the city of Kamloops. The population dwindles beyond Kamloops, and the highway steers along past Cariboo settlements like 100 Mile House and 150 Mile House, the numbers in their names representing old roadhouse distances. The gold rush to the Cariboo brought with it the development of the amazing Cariboo Wagon Road, a large portion of which is now Highway 97.

The next leg passes through Prince George, the last relatively big city you will encounter. At Dawson Creek near the Alberta border, 97 merges with the Alaska Highway. Here, the distances between towns are measured in hours of travel and the populations of settlements do not reach five digits. At the Yukon border the number of the highway changes from BC 97 to Yukon 1, although for a short distance it is the same road. Locals and tourist bureaus in these parts universally refer to the road as the Alaska Highway, and Highway 97 loses much of its identity.

Unlike many modern freeways and toll roads, Highway 97 was not built in a year. In fact, it was not even built in a decade or in a century. Highway 97 was pieced together like a long jigsaw puzzle from the historic routes in the regions it winds through. The extreme north and south ends are the latest pieces that have been added.

This book is intended to enlighten travellers about Highway 97. This old-fashioned, mostly two-lane blacktop wanders up the west side of the continent, travelling though lava beds and desert, over mountains and gorges, beside lakes, through forests and ghost towns, past rivers and gold-mining towns, and almost makes it to the Arctic. In my travels I have seen more than 200,000 kilometres (125,000 miles) of dirt, gravel and pavement pass under my tires while driving some of the world's greatest roads. I have reached the ends of the most southerly (an island in Argentina) and most northerly (Nordcap, Norway) roads on earth. I can say with pride that Highway 97, the road that runs through my neighbourhood, is the best of them all.

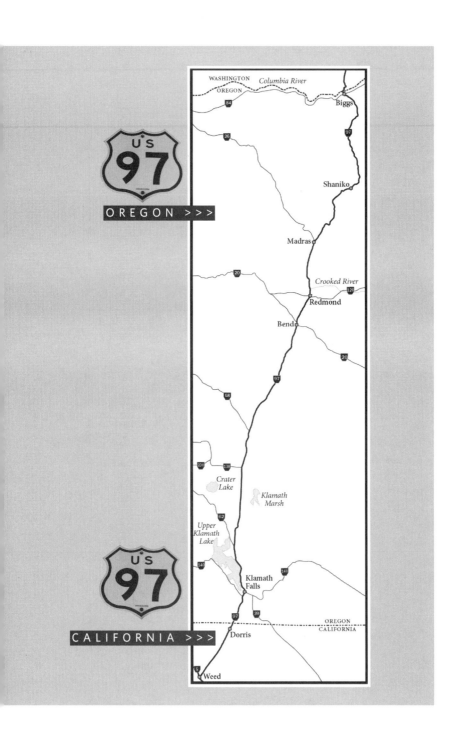

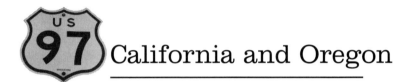# California and Oregon

OF ALL THE VARIED TERRAIN ALONG HIGHWAYS ACROSS NORTH AMERICA, few changes in scenery are as dramatic as the approach to Weed, California, as you drive northward along the giant freeway, I-5. The interstate starts at the Mexico border and rolls through the dry interior of California, past vineyards and olive groves.

At Redding, in northern California, the I-5 is just 160 metres (557 feet) above sea level, and palm trees flourish. A mere 15 minutes north, you find yourself amid snow-capped mountains and coniferous forests, travelling atop a wide highway that no longer follows a straight, dry line, but twists past beautiful waterways and towering forests.

Mount Shasta, altitude 4,317 metres (14,161 feet), is located just southeast of Weed and can be seen from 100 kilometres (62 miles) away. After California's dry, brown interior, no colour dazzles the eye as does the pristine white snow that cloaks this enormous rock, the highest volcano in the state. Seventeen trails lead to its summit and if you are extremely fit you could join the 15,000 people who make the trek every year.

When I-5 reaches the town of Weed an hour and a quarter after Redding, the road has climbed to 1,050 metres (3,457 feet). Palm trees are replaced by icy mountain streams burbling through the town. You exit from I-5 as it speeds away in search of Seattle. It is at Weed that you first set tires on my favourite highway as it twists along hillsides and soon climbs another 500 metres (1,550 feet).

 **WEED** >>> *population: 3,000*

The town of Weed (local puns: *We're high on Weed; Weed like to welcome you*) is where rural Highway 97 shakes hands with busy Interstate 5 before they go off in separate directions. The town's name has nothing to do with unwanted things that grow in the garden or that get smoked. Rather, the eponymous name comes from Abner Weed, who thought that the abundant forests, fresh water and local wind patterns would make this spot ideal for harvesting timber to mill into lumber. He built a railroad line into the area and then a spur line to his mill site.

By 1902 Weed had a mill that produced 60,000 board feet of lumber a day, as well as a post office, bunkhouse, store, box factory and several homes. Since then many mills have been built, gone out of business or burned down, but one remains in production today.

>>> The only commemorative to Highway 97 is found in Weed.

Weed is one of the few places on 97 that seems to have a sense of what the highway is all about. Though the town advertises itself as the start of the Alcan Highway this claim is somewhat flawed, since the Alcan (Alaska–Canada Highway) actually begins in Dawson Creek, B.C., nearly 2,300 kilometres (1,500 miles) north of Weed. However, the promoters of Weed (Weedites? Weeders?) can see the end from the beginning and have the only chamber of commerce or tourist bureau along the whole highway that celebrates where 97 both starts and ends.

In front of Ray's Food Place at the exit from Interstate 5 stands a stout totem pole that the tourism rep says marks the commencement of 97. Alas, there is no plaque to explain what the totem pole is all about or the reasons for the choice of a totem pole as opposed to a statue or cairn.

The explanation I received is that the highway is a link to Alaska and Alaska is famous for totem poles. A highway sign near the totem pole indicates that 97 continues south, but following that sign only leads a few kilometres along Weed Boulevard to Vista Dive and then to a dead end. This lonely spot, the very source of Highway 97, is marked only by a small cluster of gas stations. A sign advertises land for sale; no doubt this is the spot for future motels and impersonal eateries, but I hope Weed resists the temptation to lose its individuality.

<<< The very start—or end —of Highway 97.

Scenic Byways and Highways

The town of Weed proudly proclaims Highway 97 as part of the Volcanic Legacy Scenic Byway, one of just 27 All American Roads in the whole United States, chosen for their unique geography or history. This 800-kilometre (500-mile) byway links a series of Cascade Range volcanoes from California's Mount Lassen to Oregon's Crater Lake. The varied scenery along the volcano route takes in grasslands, dense forests, lava tube caves, wetlands, steaming mud pots, alpine lakes, obsidian glass flows and mountains galore. Highway 97 between Weed and Klamath Falls, Oregon, is part of the Volcanic Legacy Scenic Byway, the only section of 97 that is singled out as an America's Byway.

The US Department of Transportation labels significant roads through the America's Byways program. There are 125 America's Byways in 44 states, subdivided into 98 National Scenic Byways and 27 All American Roads. The differences between the two categories are subtle. Generally, to be named a National Scenic Byway, a road must be either historic, cultural, natural, scenic, recreational or archeological. All American Roads must possess multiple, nationally significant qualities that do not exist elsewhere. The road must be so interesting that the primary reason for a trip would be to drive along the byway. The website www.byways.org describes all the routes and offers maps and itineries.♦

The town of Weed is refreshingly quaint. Despite its location adjacent to Interstate 5, it is not a typical interchange city. No string of motels and fast-food feeders fills the cloverleaf. In fact, there are few of either and the motels that do exist are located downtown and look as if they have changed little over the past few decades. Check out the HiLo Motel's great retro neon sign.

<<< Retro signs feed those with a taste for nostalgia.

The Golden Link

Much of the history along Highway 97 is linked to the gold rushes that started in northern California in 1849 and slowly spread northward into British Columbia. The biggest gold rush in American history began 80 kilometres (50 miles) northeast of present-day San Francisco on the American River, close to Sacramento and directly south of Highway 97. James Marshall and 20 workmen were building a sawmill when, on January 24, 1848, the glint of something bright caught Marshall's eye. A year later gold fever was pandemic.

As with all gold rushes, the majority of the people who acquired wealth were not prospectors, but were rather merchants, hoteliers, suppliers, land agents and assayers who foresaw a demand for their products. Money was even made from tolls charged for travelling on the newly built roads that led to the prospecting areas.

Some prospectors mined for wealth from their hometowns. An advertisement in a Richmond, Indiana, newspaper offered a bottle of miraculous salve for $2.50. If you rubbed it all over your body, climbed up a mountain and rolled down, the gold would stick to you. By the time you reached the bottom you'd have enough gold, the ad promised, to live happily ever after. Two salves were available: one for gold and one for silver.

Tens of thousands of prospectors flooded in from the east, but westerners too were drawn to northern California by that single, mezmerizing word, gold. "In the month of July, 1848, the news of the discovery of gold in California reached Oregon," Peter Burnett wrote in *Recollections and Opinions of an Old Pioneer.* "I think that at least two-thirds of the male population of Oregon started for

A sightseeing stroll through downtown Weed takes less than an hour. The history of the town is a story of one fire after another, fuelled by mountain winds that destroyed the old wooden buildings. It is partly because of the fires that the town has evolved from a lumber town to an ecotourism town, a transition that is not uncommon along the American portion of 97. The archway at the entry to downtown is something of a throwback; it was once the style to welcome visitors by ushering them through an archway, with the name of the town or a slogan emblazoned overhead.

Attractions
Historic Lumber Town Museum
- 303 Gilman Street
- 530-938-0550

Emphasis here is on the town's early lumber industry and the railroad. The displays include hand tools that were used before electric and diesel power and larger machinery used to skid logs and to build roads through the woods. Three museum rooms have been decorated with original furniture and goods to recreate a typical kitchen, sewing room and bedroom from the 1900s. The museum also has two of the town's old jail cells and displays artifacts from a company lumber store and company hospital.

Pluto Caves, County Road A12

Mount Shasta was once an active volcano that erupted many times, sending lava into surrounding valleys. These caves are actually sections of lava tubes created when molten rock flowed through cooler outer layers. Follow Highway 97 for 12 kilometres (9 miles) north, then turn west onto County Road A12. About 2 kilometres (3 miles) along, watch for silver letters that spell out "Pluto Cave" and take that turnoff about 400 metres (or yards) to a dirt parking area. A walkway leads to the caves. A flashlight and sturdy shoes are necessary for successful spelunking.

Living Memorial Sculpture Garden
- west side of 97, 16 kilometres (10 miles) north of Weed

This collection of outdoor art pays homage to American soldiers and military personnel who have been sent to war. It is designed as a place for peace and contemplation.

Events
Carnevale
- Bel Air Park on College Avenue
- third weekend in July

For more than 50 years the mid-July weekend has been devoted to a downtown parade as well as bocce tournaments, carnival rides and food booths.

Visitor Info
- 34 Main Street, in a log cabin beside the archway
- 530-938-4624, 877-938-4624
- www.weedchamber.com

On the Road to Dorris

Leaving Weed, 97 partly follows the old Applegate Trail, an offshoot of the famous Oregon Trail that brought wagon trains from the east. When homesteaders veered south, the Applegate Trail took them to Siskiyou County, California, home of Mount Shasta.

Going north, Highway 97 continues to climb and the terrain shifts between high desert and coniferous forest. After 20 kilometres (12 miles) you enter Klamath Forest. Within 30 kilometres (20 miles) the road ascends to 1,555 metres (5,101 ft.) at

California in the summer and fall of 1848."

Hitting the trail for California took many Oregon men along a route that later became part of Highway 97. Oregon's early fame, however, came from another trail that wound its way from the east. The 3,472 kilometre (2,170 mile) Oregon Trail was opened by fur traders in the 1830s and later used by settlers heading west to the rich farmland of the Willamette Valley. Then, for 20 years beginning in 1841, 300,000 gold prospecting adventurers made the five-month journey on the trail, which started in Independence, Missouri, and ended at Oregon City, Oregon.

South from Oregon, a foot trail was the ticket for those who could not afford to go by ship or stagecoach between Portland and Sacramento. Men who had walked or ridden pack animals westward for five months didn't see the relatively short final trek to the California goldfields as too difficult.

After gold-rush fever died down in California, amid ensuing rushes at such Oregon locales as Rouge River, Jackson Creek and Applegate, prospectors retraced their steps, beating down paths between the western Coast (and Cascade) mountains and the Sierra Nevadas and plateaus to the east. Initially, the narrow paths accommodated pack horse convoys, but as more supplies were needed they were widened for carts and stagecoaches. These were the trails that marked the birth of a route that would one day grow up to become Highway 97. ◆

Grass Lake Summit, but this isn't the highest point you will reach. Just ahead is Mount Hebron Pass, which at 1,585 metres (5,202 ft.) is the loftiest point on all of 97. Get out of your vehicle, run around and see how quickly you get out of breath in the thin air. In summer the temperature here is likely to be several degrees lower than sweltering Redding. In winter it is positively frigid—colder than lower-elevation towns many hundreds of miles farther north.

After the pass you descend into Butte Valley and the Butte Valley National Grassland towards the hamlet of Macdoel, 25 kilometres (15 miles) before the Oregon border.

MACDOEL >>> *population: 600*

The village of Macdoel is known for one thing—the chariot races that are held on Sunday afternoons during the winter. The event is similar to harness racing with a horse pulling a sulky/chariot and rider. The races at Macdoel Downs have been run for three decades on a quarter-mile track. Follow the signs along Sheep Mountain Road.

Should you decide to explore the town, founded in 1906, you will find a total of two gas stations, several mini-marts, a restaurant, a truck scale and two potato-packing plants.

DORRIS >>> *population: 900*

If you look skyward about 80 kilometres (50 miles) north of Weed and see an enormous flag waving above the treetops, you have reached

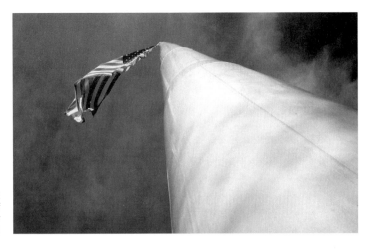

>>> You won't miss Dorris if you look for the big flag.

Dorris. Here our highway makes a couple of jogs as it meanders through the settlement.

Residents of Dorris boast that the flagpole is the tallest west of the Mississippi. The 65-metre (200-foot) pole holds a Stars and Stripes measuring 20 by 10 metres (60 by 30 feet). It is dedicated to the veterans of the many wars that America has fought.

This tiny settlement is also known for its bird life. There are two ornithological contingents that regularly visit Dorris: one shoots birds with guns, the other with cameras. The village is on a migratory flight path and it offers lots of wading water for the fowl. Cranes, swans and white pelicans all pass through and the 200 migratory species includes the largest concentration of wintering bald eagles in the lower 48 states. Highway 97 follows this avian landing zone as you head north into Oregon.

Those who hunt with cameras or guns also have an opportunity here to shoot antelope, deer, bear, wild boar, quail, pigeons, ducks and geese.

Presley Dorris settled here in 1862 and the old Dorris ranch still stands—go east on 4th Street and over the hill to the D Ranch.

Recommended Rest

Normally, overnight accommodation is not a part of this guide, but here I will make an exception. The Hospitality Inn Bed and Breakfast (200 S. California Street, 530-397-2097) is the site of the former Dorris Hospital. Remnants of the original hospital are still intact, including the upstairs maternity ward (with viewing window) and the x-ray room. The B&B was established in 1983 after a complete renovation of the old building to return it to its Victorian roots. A more interesting place to spend the night is hard to find.

Adios to California's Country Roads

Let's look to California for a quick picture of what is happening to those old, familiar roads that once wound past lakes, curved around mountains and crawled through the centres of sleepy towns.

Familiar black-and-white shields mark the friendly US highways such as 97 that preceded the growth of huge, hurried interstates. In 1962 California had just a few interstate highways, plus 23 US highways. Ten years later only 8 truncated US highways remained and 20 interstates were either completed or in the works.

Some of the old California US highways are easy to find, but in many cases they have been modified or, like sections of US 99, buried under the interstates. Others have been swallowed up, renamed and transformed. Only seven US highways still exist in California and only three—95, 97 and 199—have remained unchanged. Three more—50, 101 and 395—are fated to become superhighways. Population growth, the culture of the car and our speeded-up lives (and vehicles) have all sadly contributed to the demise of the country road. Consider that the road less travelled might be the more pleasant route to where you're headed. ♦

Events

Art in the Park, City Park

On the third weekend in August, arts and crafts are displayed and square dance demonstrations and instruction are held.

Tourist Info

- 304 S. Main Street
- 530-397-3711
- www.buttevalleychamber.com

On the Road to Klamath Falls

After waving goodbye to the fluttering flag over Dorris, Highway 97 continues its highland ways and, without fanfare, leaves California in its wake. Watch for several wildlife refuges along this stretch. Since Macdoel, Highway 97 has run parallel to the Klamath Basin birding trail. About 80 percent of the waterfowl on the Pacific Flyway funnel through this basin and the 500-kilometre (300-mile) strip of nature trail.

 KLAMATH FALLS >>> *population: 20,000*

Of all the cities along Highway 97, Klamath Falls features one of the largest and most vibrant downtown areas. Its size is a bit of a mystery in a town with a population of slightly less than 20,000 people. The biggest city on Highway 97, Kelowna, B.C., has five times as many people and a downtown of roughly the same size. Highway 97 runs right through Klamath Falls and, joy of joys, does not thrust visitors into a look-alike strip of commercial copycats. Klamath Falls does not have a huge outlying shopping district—one reason that the downtown prospers. Another is that the downtown is both pretty and pleasant.

Trees, stylish lampposts, red brick buildings, interesting businesses plus geothermally heated sidewalks that melt winter snow make Klamath Falls a pleasant place to stroll, summer or winter. Enhancing the experience are two area lakes and a river that meanders through town. If downtown strolling isn't your cup of tea you can hop on the Linkville Trolley, a rubber-tired replica of an old streetcar. A return trip within the town limits is one dollar. No wonder the downtown is alive.

Don't search for the falls on your visit. There never were any, just a series of rapids that whetted the imagination of early explorers. For years Klamath Falls was forest-industry based, a sector that has evolved into value-added businesses such as door manufacturing. There is still lumber milling in town, but agriculture (irrigation canals run beside 97 south of the city) has become a major employer. Ranching and cash crops such as pototoes and barley contribute to the agricultural industy. Government and tourism also thrive here; Klamath Falls is the seat of Klamath County. The name, by the way, comes from the Native tribe that inhabited this area, the Klamath Indians.

The Klamath yearly average of 300 days of sun adds to the joy of class-four whitewater rafting on the Klamath River, cycling a rail trail or viewing the population of wintering bald eagles. These are typical of the numerous outdoor attractions in the area. Wait for one of those 65 overcast days to go spelunking in Lava Beds National Park.

Many people visit Klamath Falls for the multitude of aquatic activities, including kayaking on the river right in the city and boating on the two lakes on the edge of town. The Link River flows through Klamath Falls and joins Lake Ewauna. Just upriver is huge Upper Klamath Lake. The city sits on the southern shore of the Upper Klamath Lake, nestled in the Klamath Basin on the eastern slopes of the Cascade Mountains.

Attractions
Birding

Birdwatching is a major pastime among both locals and tourists. It all starts on Main Street on the bridge over the Link River where buffleheads, grebes, swans, white pelicans and a multitude of other web-footed swimmers come and go with the seasons. The Klamath Basin contains at least eight wildlife refuges and sanctuaries that are ideal for birdwatching, as 350 species are said to inhabit this region.

The area contains vital stopover, nesting and refuelling sites for the migratory waterfowl travelling the Pacific Flyway. Photographers can patiently wait for that perfect shot by reserving bird blinds, and signed driving routes follow some of the refuge boundaries. Canoers and kayakers can access the Upper Klamath canoe trail that runs for 16 kilometres (9.5 miles) in four distinct segments.

Collier State Park Logging Museum
- 45 kilometres (27 miles) north of Klamath Falls on 97
- 541-783-2471

Located at the entrance to the state park on the west side of the highway, this outdoor museum illustrates the history of the logging industry. Normally, museums are found close to cities but this one, being about trees, is where it should be—next to the forest. About 50 heavy machines of both old and recent vintage are displayed and described. Additionally, there is a display of chainsaws, a blacksmith shop, tugboat, assorted steam engines, wagons, skids, tractors, sawmill equipment, a locomotive and a pioneer village with a dozen buildings. It all makes for an interesting couple of hours for those who like machines. Devoted historians could easily spend a day.

The museum itself is nearly 60 years old, dating back to 1947, when the Collier brothers donated a

---

Counting the Days of Sunshine

Klamath Falls claims "300 days of sunshine each year" and many other cities between here and the Canadian border make similar claims. Dorris, an exception, claims just 275. Without a doubt Klamath Falls has a delightful climate with lots of sun, but just to clarify the claim I asked if a day of sunshine is one hour or the entire day, from sunrise till sunset. No one yet has been able to tell me. Some research on the web provides an answer: "There is no official definition of 'days of sunshine.'"

All I need to know about climate is the number of hours of sunshine for January and for July. Toss in the annual rainfall figures and a temperature graph and that gives a pretty good picture of the weather. No additional hype or guesswork required. ♦

<<< You can explore the history of tree felling right beside the highway.

collection of antique logging equipment that they thought should be preserved. If the outdoor museum does not interest you, take a walk through the adjacent campground to where the Williamson River and Spring Creek converge. Follow a walking trail to the dramatic source of Spring Creek.

Cycling

Those who enjoy pedaling rather than paddling will be enthralled by Oregon's longest linear park. The 160-kilometre (100-mile) rail-to-trail site follows the old rail bed of the Oregon, California and Eastern Railroad (OC&E) starting at Washburn Way in Klamath Falls and wandering, adjacent to roads and rivers, to Sycan Marsh. The first 12 kilometres (8 miles) are paved and after that the trail has a rougher, graded and rolled surface. Short sections can be accessed by road. A brochure on the OC&E Woods Line State Trail is available at the tourist info stop on Main Street.

Favell Museum

- 125 W. Main Street
- 541-882-9996

Western heritage is the focus of this private institution dedicated "to the Indians who roamed and loved this land ... and to those artists who truly portray the inherited beauty which surrounds us. Their artifacts and art are an important part of the heritage of the West." Arrowheads by the bushel and thousands of intricate sculptures and paintings can be found here. When I asked the proprietor how many individual items were on display, she simply rolled her eyes. Sculpture, woodcarving, Native clothing, beadwork and tools all illustrate the skill and creativity of local Native cultures.

>>> The Favell Museum presents western heritage.

Fort Klamath Museum
- on the road to Crater Lake from Klamath Falls
- 541-381-2230

Built in 1863, the fort was the first military outpost in the region. All that is left is the guardhouse, which exhibits relics from the fort and pictures from that era. Modoc Chief Captain Jack and three warriors were hung at the fort for fighting against the US Army. Their gravesites are a short distance from the museum. The road between here and Klamath Falls was the main trade route before highway 97 was constructed. Stop in at the museum on a trip to Crater Lake.

Klamath Belle Paddlewheeler
- 541-883-4622

The *Klamath Belle* made its debut on Klamath Lake in July 2000, marking the return of a boating era that disappeared more than 75 years ago. From April through November, the 21-metre (65-foot) replica sidewheeler plies Oregon's largest natural freshwater lake. Lunch and dinner tours are on the menu as are special events such as an ice cream social on Sundays.

Klamath County Museum

- 1541 Main Street
- 541-883-4208

This old armoury, with a touch of art deco, is architecturally similar to hundreds of others built across the land. In the 1930s it hosted performances by many of America's jazz greats. Now it displays a little bit of everything, from bird life to settler artifacts and Native paraphernalia, including footwear that is 10,000 years old. Considering that the city has several other museums, the county museum is amazingly large. In 2004 it celebrated its 50th anniversary.

Lava Beds National Monument

- Tulelake, CA
- 530-667-8100

Accessible from either Dorris or Klamath Falls, the highlight of this park is the lava tube caves. Bring a light with a durable plastic lens and a coat or sweater—it's cool in the caves. You'll learn all about the volcanic eruptions that created an incredibly rugged landscape punctuated by cinder cones, lava flows, spatter cones, lava tube caves and pit craters. You'll also learn what these terms mean.

Ross Ragland Theater

- 218 N. 7th Street
- 888-627-5484

Once a 1940s movie palace, the stylish, art-deco performing arts centre is a landmark in downtown Klamath Falls. The Ragland's six-storey tower, brightly lit with neon, is a friendly beacon for travellers looking for live entertainment.

Senator George Baldwin Hotel

- 31 Main Street
- 541-883-4207

The 1906 hotel is preserved as a museum with rooms furnished as they were when it opened. Guides narrate the story of the hotel and the town. Built to lodge travellers arriving by train from San Francisco, the hotel originally had a hardware store on its main floor. Growing demand for overnight lodging prompted Senator Baldwin to remove the store and add rooms. Baldwin's daughter, Maud, left a pictorial history, which is displayed at the museum along with thousands of artifacts from that era.

Upper Klamath Lake

About 50 kilometres (30 miles) long and 13 kilometres (8 miles) wide, Upper Klamath Lake is claimed by locals to be the largest body of fresh water west of the Rockies—perhaps they didn't notice all those big lakes in British Columbia. Upper Klamath Lake hosts windsurfers, sailors, anglers and hunters as well as a highly nutritious strain of algae, *aphanizomenon flos-aquae*. This single-celled organism enjoys the warm water and is rich in micronutrients. The blue-green algae is harvested, dried and sold as a food supplement.

Events

Civil War Days and Old Fashioned Country Faire

- Fort Klamath Military Post on Highway 62
- late August

An old-style country fair with booths, food, crafts and demonstrations to supplement Civil War re-enactments.

Downtown Walk About

- third Thursday each summer month

Downtown comes alive with free trolley rides, street music, children's activities, dancing, refreshments and wine and beer tasting. Local artists demonstrate skills such as airbrush painting and jewellery making.

Horse Packing and Wilderness Skills

- at the Fairgrounds Event Center
- three days, early May weekend

With more than 110 vendors, 50 seminars, a trade show and numerous demonstrations, this big show is into its 20th year.

Klamath County Fair

- Klamath County Fairgrounds
- early August

Highlights are animal exhibits, carnival with midway, food booths, live entertainment, rodeo and demolition derby.

Tourist Info

Great Basin Visitor Association

- 507 Main Street
- 800-445-6728
- www.ci.klamath-falls.or.us or www.greatbasinvisitor.info

 DETOUR >>> **CRATER LAKE**

Anyone travelling on this portion of 97 should definitely take the short deviation to Crater Lake. Highway 97 is part of the Volcanic Legacy Scenic Byway All American Road, to give it its full cumbersome title. At Klamath Falls, Highway 140 separates from 97, heads around the west side of Upper Klamath Lake and carries the Scenic Byway designation with it. Highway 97 follows the east side of the lake, but soon intersects with number 62, where a left turn puts you on another route to Fort Klamath and Crater Lake. The majestic road circles Crater Lake and you can take number 138 back to Highway 97 and emerge just south of the town of Chemult, 50 kilometres (29 miles) from Crater Lake.

The lake was formed by the collapse of an ancient volcano, posthumously called Mount Mazama. A violent eruption 42 times as powerful as the recent eruption of Mount St. Helens occurred 7,700 years ago. The basin, or caldera, was formed after the top 1,524 metres (5,000 feet) of the volcano collapsed. Lava flows sealed the bottom, allowing the caldera to fill with water, creating the deepest lake in the United States, the seventh deepest in the world (640 metres or 1,932 feet). Rolling mountains, volcanic peaks and evergreen forests surround the lake, which on summer days almost glows with its remarkable blueness. From late October to June the cloak of snow that encircles the lake adds a backdrop for the outstanding colours.

On the Road to Bend

Past Klamath Falls the highway follows the edge of Upper Klamath Lake. The extensive marshes on either side of the road form a great birdwatching habitat. Continue north about 35 kilometres (21 miles) to both the junction to Crater Lake and the Collier Logging Museum, which is definitely worth a stop.

You are now travelling on one of the longest, straightest stretches of Highway 97. At moderately high elevations of 1,000 metres (3,300 feet) or slightly more, it sweeps through stunted coniferous forests, rarely going up, down, left or right. About 110 kilometres (68 miles) from Klamath Falls you reach Chemult, population 400, an uninspiring strip of motels and gas stations.

Thirty kilometres (20 miles) later, the settlement of Crescent, population 1,200, vanishes in your rearview mirror, as does LaPine, population 6,000, both more or less Chemult clones. Should you be in this area in winter the big events of the year are the dogsled races. The Atta Boy World Dog Sled Championship was held in several locations along Highway 97 in 2005.

For a short time, 97 is part of Oregon's Cascade Lakes Scenic Byway, a 160-kilometre (100-mile) loop formerly known as Century Drive. The scenic route follows Highway 46 into the mountains and is closed from mid-November to late May because of heavy snow. Highway 97 returns to its habit of following a curving landscape as it approaches Bend, about three hours of driving time past Klamath Falls.

 **BEND** >>> *population: 67,000*

If a competition were held for the prettiest downtown on Highway 97, Bend would be a strong contender, perhaps even the winner. It is vibrant, interesting, friendly, enthusiastic, clean and, best of all, it's beside the Deschutes River ("river of falls" in French) where it widens into Mirror Pond. The city's name comes from the twist in the waterway. Bend was formerly called Farewell Bend but the post office thought the colourful moniker too cumbersome and said farewell to Farewell. Walking and biking trails follow the river's banks only a few steps from the city core, and coffee houses offer places of contemplation and refreshment.

The stores in the downtown core all have individual character—a host of galleries and boutiques tended by loving hands. Alleyways with overhanging sculptures lead to Mirror Pond, while restaurants and bars attract a flood of customers.

There are no boarded-up buildings, no pawn shops next to instant cash stores, no lonely For Sale signs, and the streets are notably free of panhandlers and vagrants. All the residents seem happy in their jobs, and why wouldn't they be? The climate is idyllic, with just enough

<<< Mirror Pond and walking paths are behind the shops in down-town Bend.

rain to allow the trees to grow and differentiate it from the neigh-bouring desert. An altitude of 1,105 metres (3,628 feet) cools the summers, yet it is not cold enough to put snow on the ground until late December when the average daily high is still several degrees above freezing. Rivers, lakes, mountains, deserts, forests, caves, ski slopes and marshes are all at hand. If you use literature and the Internet to search for the best small American towns in which to live, the name Bend inevitably pops up.

In recent years Bend, like many of the other cities along Highway 97, has changed from an agriculture- and lumber-based economy to one grounded in ecotourism and outdoor activities. It is a logical tran-sition, since nearby there is a whole world of natural recreation. The vast range of outdoor activities in the area includes kayaking, fishing, mountain climbing, rock hounding, spelunking (technically not out-doors!) snowmobiling, birdwatching, river rafting and golf. Whether the tourism industry can employ as many people as a lumber mill is debatable, but it does make for very pleasant surroundings.

Unlike many towns along the 97 corridor in the United States, Bend is growing rapidly and property prices are rising as people re-locate from cities or come seeking retirement homes.

Attractions
Deschutes Historical Center
- 129 N.W. Idaho Street
- 541-389-1813

This relatively large museum features prehistoric and pioneer artifacts that highlight logging, irrigation, education and technology. Lodged in an old stone schoolhouse near downtown, the museum comes by its education theme naturally. Visitors can view an early 20th century schoolroom complete with desks and other equipment in use at that time, as well as typical dress worn by teachers and students.

High Desert Museum

- 59800 S. Highway 97
- 541-382-4754

Just south of Bend on the east side of the highway, set back from the road, a graceful, modern building houses a museum that interprets the local high desert. While the entry fee is high at $12, if you are going to visit just one museum on Highway 97, this should be it. It has a bit of everything, all beautifully displayed and elegantly interpreted.

>>> Exhibits are beautifully displayed in the High Desert Museum's spacious galleries.

Most of the exhibits are in the main building and include creatures of the desert, Native history, a replica of a 19th-century library, fine-arts displays and an early stagecoach. Outdoors, which is the best place for a desert museum, a sawmill, mustang corral, 1869 cabin, pond, wildlife observation area and lots of living creatures such as otter, owl, fish, raptors and porcupine will keep you busy. In the summer, the sawmill cuts wood, cowboys demonstrate their skills, stories are told, musicians play and the whole place is alive with activities.

Mount Bachelor

- 13000 S.W. Century Drive
- 800-829-2442

Mount Bachelor is 35 kilometres (22 miles) southwest of Bend on the scenic Cascades Lakes Highway. The mountain provides big-time skiing, with 10 lifts and 1,000-metre (3,100-foot) vertical drop. In late spring the lifts begin taking non-skiers to the 3,000-metre

(9,065-foot) summit for miraculous views of three states and the Cascade mountain range. There are picnic sites, barbecue pits and mountain-bike rentals in the summer months.

Newberry National Volcanic Monument

• 16 kilometres (10 miles) south of Bend on Highway 97

This national park preserves unique geologic landforms and other natural features within its 22,500 hectares (55,500 acres), and it is the only national monument on Highway 97. Newberry has several sections located on both sides of 97. As you drive along you are actually within a 44-square-kilometre (17-square-mile) caldera that is at the summit of a 1,300-square-kilometre (500-square-mile) volcano. The volcano appears dormant, but it is actually active and the activity can be measured both seismically and geothermally. Fortunately the seismic action is not strong enough to cause rumblings under your tires. Geologists say this caldera sits over a shallow magma body only 2 to 5 kilometres (3 miles) below the earth's surface.

Park highlights: Newberry Crater

• 25 kilometres (15 miles) east on Forest Service Road 21

You are in prime recreational land here, with excellent camping, fishing, hiking, mountain biking and picnicking. This area features the summit of the Newberry Volcano, two lakes and Paulina Creek Falls at the crater's western edge. An area called Big Obsidian Flow is self-explanatory. A 6-kilometre (4-mile) drive or hike on Forest Service Road 500 leads to the top of 2,600-metre (7,985-foot) Paulina Peak. You can look down at the lakes in the crater and get a better perspective on the obsidian fields and basalt flows in the surrounding area. To the far west, a picket fence of snow-clad Cascade peaks fills the horizon.

Park highlights: Lava Lands Visitor Center

• west side of 97, 18 kilometres (11 miles) south of Bend

Next to being on hand for an actual eruption, this is as good a place as any to learn about volcanoes and sample their after-effects. Lava Butte is a 7,000-year-old cinder cone with a road that spirals to the top of its 170-metre (500-foot) height and provides a view of volcanic country.

Lava Butte was formed when gas-charged molten rock sprayed volcanic cinders into the air, then fell to earth in a pile. As the eruption progressed lava poured out of the south side of Lava Butte and flowed 10 kilometres (6 miles) downhill. It's a 15-minute walk to the top of the cone, guided by some interesting and informative signage.

The visitor centre at the highway entrance offers automated displays and slide shows that describe the history of local volcanic activity. The centre is also the starting point for several interpretive trails. Benham Falls is a series of tumbling rapids just a short walk west of the centre on the Deschutes River. A footbridge crosses the river. Follow the "Deschutes River Views" signs.

The Lava Cast Forest was created when lava flowed around tree trunks. The trees disintegrated and the lava cooled leaving casts of the trees. Ask at the visitor centre for directions that will take you along a lengthy dirt road to the Lava Forest.

Events

Balloons Over Bend
• Summit High School
• 2855 N.W. Clearwater Drive and airport
• mid-June weekend

About 30 huge hot-air balloons float above Bend during this three-day annual festival. On Sunday at Bend Municipal Airport you can take a balloon ride and see model airplanes, glider demonstrations and displays.

Bend Fall Festival
• downtown streets
• early October

The harvest season is celebrated with this free community festival featuring arts and crafts, scarecrow and pumpkin decorating competitions, an open-air market, live music, and Oktoberfest celebrations with German cuisine and a beer-and-wine garden.

Cascade Festival of Music
• Drake Park
• end of August

The eight-day summer music festival is held on the banks of the Deschutes River. Throughout the week orchestral concerts offer classical works with diversions such as a Romanian Gypsy band and Cajun music.

Central Oregon Market

- Wall Street
- Saturday mornings

Artists and crafters sell their goods in an outdoor summer market in downtown Bend, across from the library.

Flashback Cruz

- downtown
- early August

For more than two decades, Cruz participants have shown antique and classic cars, muscle cars, street machines, rods and trucks built before 1974. Close to 300 classics line up in Drake Park, then cruise through downtown Bend. Sunday is a Fun Cruz to Mount Bachelor for the Car Olympics.

Sisters Rodeo

- 31 kilometres (20 miles) northwest of Bend
- mid-June weekend, town of Sisters

This rodeo has been one of the most popular on the west-coast circuit for more than 65 years. Because of the big purses and bonuses, cowboys dub the rodeo "The Biggest Little Show in the World." Saturday morning parade, Sunday pancake breakfast.

Sisters Outdoor Quilt Show

- town of Sisters
- second weekend in July

Billed as the "Largest Outdoor Quilt Show in America," the Sisters event has run for 30 years and features more than 1,000 quilts displayed throughout town. A week of events precedes the show and includes classes, textile demonstrations, art and quilting exhibits and live music.

Snowshoe Tours

- Mount Bachelor
- weekends, January through March

A Forest Service naturalist leads free snowshoe tours at Mount Bachelor. Snowshoes are provided and no previous experience is necessary. The one-hour tours start at 10 a.m. and 1:30 p.m. Meet near the West Village Guest Services building at Mount Bachelor.

WinterFest

- mid-February

Downtown festivities start Friday evening with the winter wine walk and fireworks over Mirror Pond. The festival features ice carving competitions, a children's nightlight parade, music, art and family entertainment.

Tourist Info

- 917 N.W. Harriman
- 800-949-6086
- www.ci.bend.or.us

 REDMOND >>> *population: 17,850*

Before you have a chance to adjust to the wide-open spaces north of Bend, you are upon Redmond, just 25 kilometres (15 miles) up the road. Redmond is almost an adjunct to Bend and is regarded locally as something of an underdog. Redmond citizens are quick to point out how much friendlier their city is, but unless the citizens run up, hug you and ask if they can give you money I don't see a lot of room for improvement in friendliness over Bend.

Despite the Crooked and Deschutes rivers being close by, there is nothing recreationally aquatic within Bend city limits. Water, however, was a factor in the beginnings of Redmond, as farsighted Frank Redmond bought some land where a new canal and a new railway would meet. There he pitched his tent and sat on his investment. Within a few years more settlers came and, as there was a lack of construction lumber in the area, 75 tent dwellings made up the town.

This growth came relatively late, as town development goes. Incorporated in 1910, Redmond is one of the younger cities along 97. A walking tour of historic downtown takes in buildings that are not quite a century old and do not have exceptional architectural merit. However, Redmond is a collector's paradise with its concentration of antique and collectibles shops. I didn't count them, but the city brags of 60.

Outdoor enthusiasts are drawn to Redmond as they are to Bend. Unique to the area are the dramatic spires and craggy palisades of Smith Rock State Park just off 97 north of the city. The park offers world-class climbing for neophyte and experienced climbers alike. About 15 kilometres (9 miles) north of Redmond, turn right onto N.W. Smith Rock Way and in five minutes you will reach the park.

Attractions
Crooked River Dinner Train
- 541-548-8630

This 100-passenger, 2-car excursion train sports an 1800s theme and nefarious characters from the Wild West are likely to stage a robbery. A return outing is 40 kilometres (25 miles) and leaves from Prineville Junction. Brunch and supper trips and murder mystery rides are also on offer.

Petersen Rock Garden and Museum
- 16 kilometres (9 miles) north of Bend on 97 at 61st Street

The Petersen rock garden falls short of being an international attraction, but it is so peculiar that it deserves a look. Rasmus Petersen was born in Denmark in 1883 and at age 17 he settled in Oregon. In 1906 he built a two-storey house and began collecting rocks such as Oregon agates, obsidian, petrified wood, malachite and jasper. In 1935 Petersen started using his rocks to construct miniature buildings, terraces, towers, monuments and bridges. By his death in 1952, Petersen had created a 1.6-hectare (4-acre) rock garden that is now supported by donations and a gift shop.

Reindeer Ranch: Operation Santa Claus
- Highway 126
- 541-548-8910

Two miles west of Redmond on Highway 126 the largest herd of domesticated reindeer in the United States grazes contentedly. The establishment claims to be the world's largest commercial reindeer ranch and is home to more than 100 of Santa's sleigh pullers. The ranch is open year-round for self-guided tours, and as a working-reindeer park, it provides reindeer for attractions, photography and parades across the country during the Christmas season.

Tourist Info
- 446 S.W. 7th Street
- 541-923-5191
- www.visitredmondoregon.com

On the Road to the Columbia River

On the west side of Highway 97, 13 kilometres (8 miles) past Redmond, an excellent stopping spot called the Peter Skene Ogden Scenic View Point overlooks the Crooked River. Born in Quebec in 1794, Peter Ogden was a fur trader and explorer who kept journals of his many expeditions.

From a height of 100 metres (330 feet) you can look down into the steep Crooked River canyon and walk across an old bridge that used to support Highway 97. Those who suffer from acrophobia or vertigo are advised to keep their feet planted on terra firma.

After the Crooked River, Highway 97 resumes its interesting ways, bouncing up hills and gliding through dales. The twisty terrain continues to alternate between desolate high desert and confining coniferous forest.

 MADRAS >>> *population: 5,290*

This agricultural centre, high on a windy plain, comes but a few dozen kilometres after Redmond. Madras is another relatively young city, incorporated in 1911 after successes in agriculture, lumber and the railroad.

Events
Pat's Cowdeo
• mid-October

Should you be in the Madras vicinity in the middle of October this fun event is worth catching. A peewee rodeo showcases young wannabe cowboys who compete in such junior events as sheep riding and an old-fashioned greased pig chase.

Tourist Info
• 274 S.W. 4th Street
• 541-475-2350
• 800-967-3564
• www.madraschamber.com

The next stretch of 97 has a number of interesting spots within a short distance of Madras including a ghost town, a site devoted to a family of warblers (not the avian type), a few dusty towns and the first crossing of the Columbia River.

About 55 kilometres (35 miles) past Madras, a sign beside the highway proclaims that you are crossing the 45th line of latitude—halfway between the equator and the North Pole. This is not a localized phenomenon. Millions of people in the northern part of the globe—in Europe and throughout Asia—cross this invisible line every day, but very few get to read a sign that makes them aware of their place on the planet. I like these types of signs; they add interest to the journey and enhance our usually sketchy knowledge of geography. How about some signs on east-west routes that intersect Highway 97 stating, "You are crossing the most interesting road on the continent"?

 SHANIKO >>> *population: 25*

Five kilometres (3 miles) beyond the 45th parallel sign, you suddenly encounter a conglomeration of old wooden buildings that only a sharp curve in the highway avoids. Slow down, otherwise you may enter the main street of Shaniko at 100 kilometres (60 miles) per hour and risk levelling the row of rickety, historic dwellings. The restored brick hotel might be more of a barrier, but either way you would not be a popular tourist.

Shaniko is unique among ghost towns. It sits right on the highway so you don't have to search for it along miles of dusty back roads. A trip through this western town that's partly restored and partly

<<< The ghost town Shaniko is conveniently located almost right on 97.

derelict will add no distance and not much time to your journey. Among the sights are an old jail wagon, a restored hotel and the deserted back streets with rickety wooden buildings.

During its boom days right after the turn of the last century, this railhead town claimed the title "Wool Capital of the World." In 1910 the population was 600 and the residents supported five saloons, three hotels, a bank, blacksmith shops, two newspapers, a post office, school, stores and other businesses. Some of the 1900s-era buildings still stand, but the heart of the town burned down in a series of fires.

Today the town's 25 residents farm and also operate the big, restored Shaniko Hotel and the post office, campground, general store and collectibles store. The hotel was reopened in 2001 and is owned by philanthropist and businessman Dr. Robert B. Pamplin Jr., who also owns the 55,000-acre R2 Ranch next to Highway 97.

Tourist Info

• www.shaniko.com, www.pamplin.org

Beyond Shaniko you enter a section of road designated as an Oregon Scenic Byway, but honestly, this is not the most scenic part of either Oregon or Highway 97. While the hilly, forested terrain makes for a very pleasant drive, I question its being designated as singularly scenic.

The occasional community dots the shoulders of this largely unpopulated countryside and next up is Kent, 25 kilometres (15 miles) past Shaniko. Kent has the distinction of having the smallest population of any signed settlement along 97, with 23 residents. Kent appears destined to become another ghost town, and a few zealous books and websites list it as one. Note the old gas station wasting away on the east side of the road, closed when the owners couldn't afford to bring it up to environmental protection standards. It would be nice to see it restored to its 1950s glory.

Another 20 kilometres (12 miles) brings you to Grass Valley, population 170, with a huge antique/junk store and the shortest bicycling lane (half a kilometre, or three-tenths of a mile) I've ever seen. Travellers approaching from the north will see, painted on the side wall of a store, the words "Last Groceries for 67 Miles."

Moro, with a population of less than 400, comes next. The community has a pleasant museum devoted to local history. The Sherman

<<< Grass Valley makes the best of its isolation.

County Historical Museum (200 Dewey Street, 541-565-3232) has a room of special interest to Highway 97 afficionados, dedicated to explaining the roads and trails that are related to and connected with the Oregon Trail.

Moro also sports a pair of huge antique stores that are worth a visit for those who like treasure hunting. A devoted collector or eBay seller could easily spend half a day rooting through the disordered shelves of dusty collectibles.

DeMoss Memorial Park

Tucked in a valley about 35 kilometres (20 miles) before the Washington border sits an unusual and very pleasant picnic site with a story to tell. A sign gives the full title of this spot as Sherman County's DeMoss Memorial Park. The park commemorates the DeMoss Lyric Bards, a local singing family that performed for audiences around the world. The DeMoss parents and their five talented children toured from 1872 through 1933 but called this spot, where they had planned a townsite, home. Swings, tables, a spring and the remains of a stage upon which the family performed make the park a cut above your average rest spot.

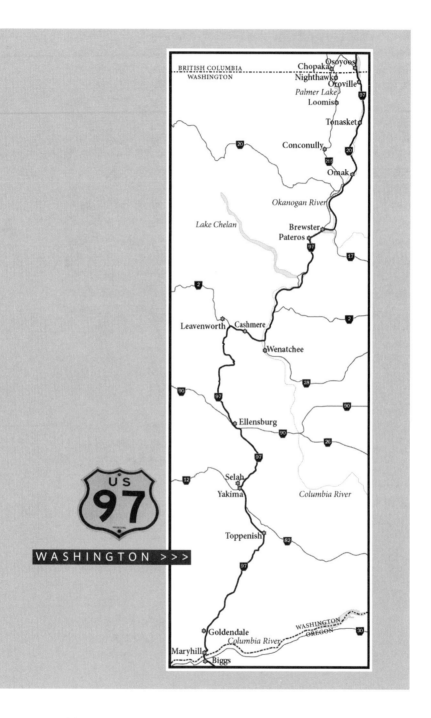

WASHINGTON >>>

CHAPTER TWO

# Washington

ATOP SEVERAL RISES YOU CAN SEE, ON A CLEAR DAY, Mount Adams to the north and Mount Hood to the west. The Columbia River—the first significant water since Crooked River—forms the Oregon/ Washington border and the highway plunges into a cluster of gas stations on the Oregon side (a few cents a gallon cheaper) and then ascends into Washington. As you climb out of the gorge, sharp eyes will pick out a structure on the right that looks very much like England's Stonehenge, overlooking the north side of the river.

 **MARYHILL** >>> *population: 100*

Attractions
Stonehenge

This war memorial, built by a gentleman who crusaded against war, is a full-scale replica of England's famous and mysterious Stonehenge. Sam Hill, the builder, was mistakenly informed that the original Stonehenge had been used as a sacrificial site, so he built his version "to remind my fellow men of the incredible folly of still sacrificing human life to the

The Names and Numbers

The first North American inventory of roads, outside of those in cities, was conducted in 1904 with route mileage subdivided according to surface type. The report, published three years later, concluded that there were 2,151,570 miles of rural public roads in the United States and, surprisingly, 1,598 miles of stone toll roads. Only 153,662 miles of public roads were recorded as having any kind of surfacing. The remaining 2 million miles were, presumably, dirt tracks.

At the turn of the 20th century only 10,000 automobiles chugged along this continent's dusty roads. Ownership was concentrated in big cities and wealthy car owners used their vehicles mainly for pleasure. However, pleasure driving was soon restricted by a host of laws and ordinances. Many jurisdictions began charging motor vehicle registration fees, while some cities and villages levied a wheel tax for the privilege of driving on their streets.

god of war." Sam Hill is not famous for "what in the Sam Hill!" but instead was an important pioneer in road building and was instrumental in the construction of Highway 99, also known as the Pacific Highway, which once connected the Mexican and the Canadian borders. Much of it has since been taken over by I-5.

>>> Road-builder Sam Hill created the Stonehenge replica.

Sam Hill's background in railroads brought him and his family from Minneapolis to reside at the railroad terminus in Seattle in the late 1800s. Although roads and railroads were rivals, Hill recognized that on the wet and muddy coast, people and products could not make it to railroad stations without good roads.

Inspired by a 55-kilometre (34-mile) road trip that seemed to take forever, he vowed that he would build a hard-surfaced highway from the Mexican border to Vancouver, B.C. He organized the happily named Washington State Good Roads Association with the goal of creating a system of hard-surfaced roads to replace the messy, unsigned, unsurfaced assortment of private, city and county roads. Construction of the Pacific Highway through Washington started in 1913 and 10 years later it was complete.

Maryhill Museum of Art and Loops Road

In 1907 Sam Hill bought 2,400 hectares (6,000 acres) of land overlooking the Columbia River gorge for a Quaker agricultural community. Seven years later construction of his mansion began; he named it Maryhill, after his daughter, Mary. The Quaker community did not turn out to be a success, so several of his friends worked with him to turn the mansion into an art museum. Hill's castle-like mansion is located on the west side of Highway 97, 7 kilometres (4 miles) from the Stonehenge monument. The estate covers more than 10 hectares (26 acres) on both sides of the highway. An extensive collection of Sam Hill's road-related memorabilia is on permanent display in the museum.

At Maryhill, Hill built several miles of road and experimented with road-building techniques and surfacing materials. Laid down in 1913, the 5.8-kilometre (3.6-mile) Loops Road was the first paved road in the Pacific Northwest. It winds around a hillside just north of the Stonehenge monument, near the junction of routes 14 and 97.

The road was refurbished in 1998 and is open daily for bicyclists and pedestrians. Seven types of experimental road construction were employed to build Loops Road, including liquid asphalt shipped from California. Hill was passionate about getting roads built and represented Washington at the first International Road Congress in Paris in 1908.

Events
Maryhill Car Show and Loops Road Hill Climb
- mid-October weekend
- 509-773-3733

Classic, sports and customized cars gather on the lawn for a show on Saturday. The next day there is an ascending race along the Loops Road course.

On the Road to Wine and Grapes

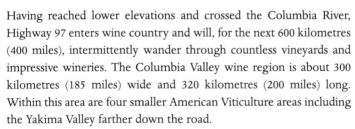

Having reached lower elevations and crossed the Columbia River, Highway 97 enters wine country and will, for the next 600 kilometres (400 miles), intermittently wander through countless vineyards and impressive wineries. The Columbia Valley wine region is about 300 kilometres (185 miles) wide and 320 kilometres (200 miles) long. Within this area are four smaller American Viticulture areas including the Yakima Valley farther down the road.

Here in Klickitat County there are about 30 wineries and vineyards. Maryhill Winery (509-773-1976, **www.MaryhillWinery.com**) is just 8 kilometres (5 miles) off Highway 97 at 9774 Highway 14 near Goldendale. Maryhill has produced fruit of all kinds since Sam Hill's arrival in the late 1800s. Picnicking is welcomed under a spacious arbour giving views of Mount Hood and the Columbia River gorge. The winery has a 4,000-seat amphitheatre, where a series of concerts runs through the summer. It has featured Bob Dylan, Willie Nelson, ZZ Top and other major performers.

 GOLDENDALE >>> *population: 3,760*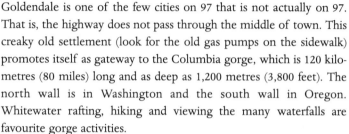

Goldendale is one of the few cities on 97 that is not actually on 97. That is, the highway does not pass through the middle of town. This creaky old settlement (look for the old gas pumps on the sidewalk) promotes itself as gateway to the Columbia gorge, which is 120 kilometres (80 miles) long and as deep as 1,200 metres (3,800 feet). The north wall is in Washington and the south wall in Oregon. Whitewater rafting, hiking and viewing the many waterfalls are favourite gorge activities.

Attractions
Goldendale Observatory State Park
• 1602 Observatory Drive, 509-773-3141

Located on a hilltop north of Goldendale, this facility caters to the public with programs designed to educate the novice as well as the experienced stargazer. A 62-centimetre (24.5-inch) telescope is used for public viewing. The Washington State Parks Department runs the facility, so camping and picnicking are available. This may be the only campground where you can both sleep under the stars and study them through a public telescope.

Presby Mansion-Klickitat Historical Society Museum
• 127 W. Broadway
• 509-773-4303

The museum is housed in the three-storey Presby Mansion, which was built in 1902. It is stocked with furniture, clothing, utensils and personal effects from the 1880s through 1930s.

On the Road to Hops and Shops

Driving on from Goldendale the Yakima Valley spreads before you, a fertile, 140,000-hectare (350,000-acre) patchwork of small farms that yield asparagus, eggplant, apricots, winter pears, mints, berries, pumpkins and about 30 other types of fruits and vegetables. Rows of trellises hold up hop bushes (bright green in season) that are used to flavour beer. Vineyards abound.

As you enter the Yakima Valley, Highway 97 changes dramatically. It becomes a four-lane, divided freeway, straight, fast and flat, that speeds past Toppenish, Union Gap, Wapato, Yakima and Selah without providing reason to gape. What you see are malls, trailer parks and the usual array of commercial strips. That's not a knock against the locals. It just seems that rarely does one want to locate anything pretty beside a concrete car conduit.

My advice here is unusual—turn your back on 97. Flirt with the byways and drive through the aforementioned towns. Toppenish has done a wonderful job of decorating with murals, Wapato is something of an economic wasteland (which makes it interesting, in a way), Union Gap is mall city (not a criticism), Yakima offers a number of interesting surprises and Selah is worth a side trip.

97 TOPPENISH >>> population: 9,000 ✔ ✔

This interesting city spouts the motto, "Where the West Still Lives," and it lives by its words. The streets have a western flair, and the restored buildings sport overhangs that shade the sunny sidewalks and provide inspiration to pause, sit on a bench and talk to a stranger.

If that motto should ever turn stale, Toppenish has a backup: "City of Museums and Murals." On 60 of the city's walls, colourful murals depict the history of the community. Some are so expertly painted that they blend in with the surroundings and, at a glance, one assumes them to be a part of the landscape. In summer a horse-drawn covered wagon takes visitors on a mural tour. There is even a mural-related shop where you can purchase postcards, calendars and books of the artwork. Highway 97's two mural cities, Toppenish and Vernon, B.C., in the north Okanagan, are a bit of a study in contrasts. Vernon, a bigger city, has close to the same number of murals but does not promote them nearly as enthusiastically as does Toppenish.

This area also has a fine variety of unique museums, including one dedicated to the hops crop. Hop cones are used to preserve and flavour beer and are an important Yakima Valley agricultural product. In fact, according to local lore, 75 percent of American hops are grown in this area.

The name Toppenish comes from the Native word *Thappahn-ish*, meaning "people of the trail from the hills."

Attractions
American Hop Museum
- 22 S. B Street
- 509-865-4677

The only museum on the continent dedicated to displaying the history of the perennial vine *Humulus lupulus* serves up a unique educational experience. The exhibits tell you just about everything you might want to know about hops. The stone building itself is beautiful. Note the *trompe l'oeil* motif painted high on the outside walls. If you look closely you will see the optical illusion. In 1917 this building was the Trimble Brothers Creamery.

>>> The only museum dedicated to hops is in Toppenish.

Central Washington Agricultural Museum
- 4508 Main Street, Union Gap
- 509-457-8735

Set on 6 hectares (15 acres) of farmland just north of Toppenish, this museum is for agrarians and aficionados of frontier farming. There may very well be 1,000 or more tractors, plows, harvesters, drills, threshers, planters and things that go bump on the land. Many are not labelled, so you had better know your machinery or simply have an appreciation of old farm equipment. If you do, you will love this massive collection. There are numerous barns, a log cabin, railcar and other dwellings. Climb the hill for a view that will put the whole thing into perspective.

Fort Simcoe State Park
- near the village of White Swan
- 30 kilometres (20 miles) west of Toppenish along Route 220

An 80-hectare (200-acre) park in an old oak grove watered by natural springs, Fort Simcoe was an 1850s-era military installation. It is one of the oldest settlements along Highway 97. The fort was built in the late 1850s, after the Yakama Indian Wars, and used for only three years. Five original furnished buildings are still standing: the commander's house, three captains' houses and a blockhouse. Various other buildings have been recreated. Prior to 1850, the site was used as a trade centre

<<< The agricultural museum has six hectares of farm equipment on display.

and campground for the Native American bands that make up the Yakama Indian Nation.

Gibbon's Pharmacy Soda Fountain
- S. Toppenish Street, centre of town

This traditional 1950s soda fountain is typical of what was once a part of many pharmacies. Partly recreated and partly original, it is a great place to sit at the counter on a rotating stool and sip a soda or slurp a float.

Northern Pacific Railway Museum

- 10 Asotin Avenue
- 509-865-1911

A restored telegraph shop and the 1911 Northern Pacific depot have been restored to show what an operating railway station was like in the 1930s. There is also a section house and a freight house.

Toppenish Museum

- 1 S. Elm Street
- 509-865-4510

An eclectic combination of firefighting equipment, early cattle-ranching history, Yakima Valley polo, gold panning and local wild-horse traditions are on exhibit. If you want Grampa and Grandma to tell a story to you or your kids, make an appointment.

Yakama Nation Museum

- 280 Buster Road
- 509-865-2000

The combination RV park, library, museum, restaurant, gift shop and theatre are an enterprise of the federation of 14 tribes that make up the Yakama Nation. The museum has several Native dwellings including a sweat lodge, winter lodge, tepee and summer arbour. Life-size statues of American Native leaders from the past in full costume stand watch amid the dioramas and displays of foods, tools and utensils. The campground features tepees that are available for overnight stays.

>>> Native food and lodging are offered at Yakama Nation Museum.

Events
Hoptoberfest
- Central Washington Fairgrounds' Modern Living Building
- third Saturday of October

Microbrewery displays, music, a silent auction and German cuisine are the features of this local variation of Oktoberfest.

Mural in a Day
- downtown Toppenish
- early June

A dozen artists work together to create a historically accurate mural in one day. Other arts and crafts are displayed during the event.

Washington State Pioneer Power Show
- Agricultural Museum
- third weekend of August

Restored antique farm equipment is fired up for events that include an old-time threshing bee.

Tourist Info
Yakima Valley Visitors Information Center
- exit 33A from I-82/97

This modern centre, serving all of the Valley cities, is equipped with computers for public use and can print off maps of specific areas.

 YAKIMA >>> *population: 72,000*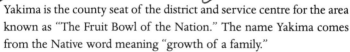

Yakima is the county seat of the district and service centre for the area known as "The Fruit Bowl of the Nation." The name Yakima comes from the Native word meaning "growth of a family."

The wine industry has taken root in this desert valley and is growing rapidly in the third largest city on Highway 97. Close to 50 wineries dot an 80-kilometre (50-mile) stretch along 97 and I-82 from Yakima to Benton City. Some are quite impressive and many offer free tasting and tours. A quick and convenient introduction to local wine can be found in the tasting room of Yakima Cellars (32 N. 2nd Street, 509-577-0461), located downtown near the Capitol Theater.

Attractions
Capitol Theater
- 19 S. 3rd Street
- 509-853-8000

Serving as Yakima's primary performing arts stage, this 90-year-old vaudeville theatre seats 1,500 and has been restored to its former glory. In 1975 an electrical fire severely damaged the theatre, but rebuilding began immediately.

Yakima Area Arboretum
- 1401 Arboretum Drive at Nob Hill Boulevard
- 509-248-7337

A tree museum that grows both native and exotic plants from around the world, the 25-hectare (62-acre) grounds feature the Waterfall Garden, Plath Solarium, Japanese Garden, greenway walking path and wetlands trail. Examine the tree exhibits at the Jewett Interpretive Center.

Yakima Greenway, along the Yakima River

The 16-kilometre (10-mile) river pathway is designed for bikers, hikers, strollers and rollers. It extends over 1,400 hectares (3,600 acres) and includes three parks, two lakes and two rivers with four river landings.

Yakima Valley Museum
- 2105 Tieton Drive
- 509-248-0747

This modern building looks like anything but a museum. And looks are not necessarily deceiving, for the inside neither looks nor feels like a museum. Take for instance the Neon Garden, a collection of neon signs. Or the operating 1930s art deco soda fountain. Or the hands-on Children's Underground activity centre. What one might expect is also available: the largest collection of wooden wagons west of the Mississippi, fruit industry history and Native artifacts.

Events
Central Washington State Fair
- Central Washington Fairgrounds
- end of September

Close to a third of a million visitors are attracted to this traditional 10-day state fair each year.

Farmers' Market
- E. Yakima Avenue and S. 3rd Street
- Sundays, 9 a.m. to 2 p.m.

Vendors from throughout the Valley bring fresh produce to sell. Entertainment and samples as well.

Luminaria
- Jewett Visitor Center
- 1401 Arboretum Drive
- early December

One thousand candles light a path around the arboretum grounds and lead to Central Washington's largest lighted Christmas tree.

 SELAH >>> *population: 6,395*

Selah is situated at the north end of the Yakima Valley and proclaims itself the "Apple Juice Capital of the World." It is the home of Tree Top Apple Juice, the self-named "world's largest apple processor." Even Kelowna's Sun Rype factory, in the heart of British Columbia's apple orchards, buys apple juice from Tree Top. But the figures don't necessarily support the company's claim as world's largest. For the past few years China has produced about 43 percent of the world's apple juice, Poland 18 percent, the United States 8 percent and Argentina 6 percent.

Tree Top is a grower-owned cooperative with 2,500 grower-owners in three states. Selah is also home to three fresh-fruit packing and storage plants. Several companies offer orchard tours and sampling.

Selah also has a hiking path that connects to the Yakima River Greenway, and is a gateway to the Yakima River canyon, a fly fishing paradise.

 ELLENSBURG >>> *population: 16,000*

Ellensburg is located near the geographic centre of Washington State. It is a distinguished city with a stately downtown that looks very much like a small turn-of-the-century city lifted right out of the movies. The historic shopping district features six blocks of late-Victorian brick buildings. The core of Ellensburg was rebuilt in 1889, mostly with

Had T.S. Eliot hopped aboard a camper and gone touring, as did John Steinbeck, he might have written about highways instead of the secret lives of frolicking felines. He may very well have penned *The Naming of Roads* and perhaps inspired *Highways* instead of *Cats*:

The naming of roads is a difficult matter

It isn't just one of your travelling games

You may think at first I'm as mad as a hatter

When I tell you, a road must have three different names.

The formal name, of course, is Highway 97. On a provincial or state level it may also be called something like the Scenic Volcanic Route, the Wine Discovery Trail or the Historical Exploration Loop. On a more casual basis, Highway 97 is additionally known as Main Street, Alaska Road or Harvey Avenue as it winds through an urban area and serves as the main thoroughfare. Maps seldom give more than one name for a road, so any confusion that all this naming and renaming might engender is understandable.

Not until 1926 did a national highway numbering system come into being in the United States. Strictly speaking, there is no national road numbering

brick, following a huge fire that levelled 10 wooden city blocks.

These "six brick blocks" include museums, art galleries, antique shops, jewellery stores, many locally owned unique clothing and gift stores, and restaurants. The century-old buildings look like they were put up yesterday. Brick sidewalks, vintage lighting and old-style signage all add to the ambience.

Aside from the old downtown, the city's most interesting attraction is the Chimposiums at Washington University's Chimpanzee and Human Communications Institute. Here resides Washoe, the signing chimp. Washoe is an icon of controversy in the psycholinguistics field for her reputed ability to use American Sign Language to converse with her chimp family and her custodians.

Attractions
Chimpanzee and Human Communication Institute

• Central Washington University
• 400 E. University Way
• 509-963-2244

The institute offers Chimposiums—one-hour educational workshops that involve the world-renowned chimpanzees who may or may not have acquired sign language vocabularies. The workshops are education rather than entertainment oriented.

Clymer Museum of Art

• 416 N. Pearl Street
• 509-962-6416

The Clymer Museum of Art showcases the spirit of pioneer life through the career of Ellensburg artist John Ford Clymer, whose historically accurate illustrations capture early western America.

Japanese Gardens

- Central Washington University
- 400 E. 8th Avenue

These authentic Japanese gardens combine the natural features of Kittitas Valley with traditional Japanese landscaping and plantings.

Kittitas County Historical Museum

- Cadwell Building
- 114 E. 3rd Avenue
- 509-925-3778

The museum's specialties are a rock collection, doll collection and Native American beaded bags and basketry. The Cadwell Building was constructed in 1889 and has unique, horseshoe-shaped windows.

Thorp Mill

- Thorp exit (#101) off I-90
- 509-964-9640

Built in 1883, the Thorp gristmill is one of the few mills left in the state and the oldest industrial artifact in Kittitas County. This four-storey gristmill, in the tiny town of Thorp, utilized Yakima River water brought via canal. A horizontal water wheel powered both the gristmill and a sawmill.

Events
Farmers' Market

- Wells Fargo Bank parking lot
- 4th and Pearl Streets

Saturday morning, May through October, downtown Ellensburg.

First Friday Artwalk

- first Friday of every month

The artwalk is a self-guided walking tour of about 20 participating galleries with rotating displays of

system in Canada. Most highways in the early 1920s had names and were identified with trailblazer signs painted on posts along the routes. By the mid-1920s, several national trails had been established by highway promotional groups. Many overlapped or had similar names and the system was confusing. The American Association of State Highway Officials came up with a numbering system for US highways in 1926 and their numbered shields slowly replaced the trailblazer markers. The association decreed that even numbers would be assigned to east-west highways, with their numbers increasing from north to south and odd-numbered highways would run north-south, increasing in number from east to west. Thus 97, a high, odd number, was assigned to a western road that went in a north-south direction.

In the 1930s British Columbia labelled its roads with letters, and the highway stretching north from Osoyoos first got a T to represent "Okanagan–North Thompson Highway," although at that time the road barely reached the South Thompson. When B.C. highways were later numbered, it was less confusing to leave the number, where practical, as it was south of the border. Thus the T highway—a continuation of US 97—became BC 97. ♦

work by local artists. Opening nights take place in each venue from 5 to 7 p.m.

Spirit of the West Cowboy Gathering
- various locations
- early February
- 888-925-2204

A celebration of western music, poetry and art. There are close to 40 different events with 30 entertainers.

Tourist Info
- Ellensburg Chamber of Commerce
- 609 N. Main Street
- 888-925-2204
- **www.ellensburg-chamber.com**

On the Road to Apples and Juice

Leaving Ellensburg, Highway 97 takes a jaunt to the west, turns north and passes through Wenatchee National Forest, a site with some excellent camping and hiking. It then goes over Blewett Pass at 1,280 metres (4,100 feet), joins Highway 2 and travels beside the Wenatchee River into the town of Wenatchee. At the point where 97 joins number 2, a turn to the west leads to Leavenworth, less than 10 kilometres (6 miles) from the junction.

 LEAVENWORTH >>> *population: 2,500*

This picturesque tourist town in the mountains sports a Bavarian theme that goes beyond architecture. Many store clerks and residents dress in traditional Bavarian costumes. Christmas lights are a major winter attraction and the German-style town is a cool spot in the heat of summer, so this area can be a crowded place in both seasons. Leavenworth offers an assortment of outdoor activities such as hiking, horseback riding and biking, plus the usual indoor shopping and dining. However, the most popular draws are the Bavarian architecture and the mountain scenery.

The town began as a rail centre, evolved into the lumber business and then died during the Depression when 24 empty stores lined the two-block town centre. In the 1960s the citizens decided they had to

<<< An abandoned farmhouse near Wenatchee.

do something to revive the town. Swayed by the backdrop of alpine hills they turned the town into a Bavarian village. To make the theme more meaningful than simply a facelift of the buildings, the community banded together to create foods, festivals, music and dress to represent a credible Bavarian mountain village.

Events
Icefest
• middle of January

Included are "Schmooshing" dog-sled races, a coloured-ice-cube hunt, skiing, fireworks and sleigh rides.

International Choral Festival
• mid-April
• 509-662-2397

This annual festival features up to eight choral groups from Washington and British Columbia.

Spring Bird Festival
• early May weekend

Bird identification and song, plus the study of geology, wildflowers and conservation are all part of the festivities. Art exhibits showcase local talent and a songbird concert at Canyon Wren Recital Hall caps off the weekend. Guided trips and activities range from leisurely strolls to energetic hikes, and most are free.

Bavarian Maifest

• weekend close to May 1

Maifest takes you back in time, with 16th-century costumes, games, dancing, jousting, eating, drinking, oompahpah music and general revelry in old Bavarian style. Included is the traditional dance that takes place around the village Maipole.

International Accordion Celebration

• one week in mid-June

The celebration of accordion music includes jazz, popular, classical, ethnic and other styles. There are workshops, jam sessions, a parade and four nights of concerts.

Oktoberfest

• first week of October

The traditional German festival features bands in the Festhalle, plus German food, beer and a parade.

Christmas lighting

• first, second and third weekends of December

Visitors come by the busloads for Leavenworth's most famous festival. On weekdays the dark town awaits Saturday's light up and festivities. At dusk everyone gathers to sing "Silent Night" and witness the lighting of the village.

Tourist Info

• 509-548-5807
• www.leavenworth.org

 CASHMERE >>> *population: 2,714*

This settlement on the Wenatchee River was originally called Mission, but had to abandon the name because there was already a Mission in Washington State. Instead it became Cashmere, as it reminded a local judge of Kashmir, India, also a foothills area.

As well as sharing its location as the geographic centre of the state with Selah, Cashmere calls itself "Tree City USA." The town gets a bit more rain than other areas along this part of 97, and the Wenatchee River provides irrigation, so stately trees adorn the many parks.

Attractions
Cashmere Pioneer Village and Museum
- 600 Cotlet Way
- 509-782-3230

Twenty original, furnished pioneer buildings recreate homesteading in the 1800s, with railway cars, a water wheel and Native American artifacts. A surprisingly big pioneer village for such a small community.

Liberty Orchards Applets and Cotlets Candy Kitchen
- 117 Mission Avenue
- 509-782-4088

You can watch fruit and nut treats being made by hand in essentially the same way as in 1920. Washington apples are combined with English walnuts to get applets, and apricots are combined with walnuts to produce cotlets. The ingredients are slow-simmered together to condense the flavours. Liberty provides free tours and samples.

Events
Apple Days
- first weekend of October at Cashmere Pioneer Village

Among the many events are a pie auction, pie walk, pie baking contest, bake sale, magicians, musicians and the sheriff and his deputies having shoot-outs with robbers at the saloon.

Tourist Info
- 301 Angier Avenue #B
- 509-782-0708
- www.visitcashmere.com

 WENATCHEE >>> *population: 34,508*

The descent into the warm Wenatchee River Valley brings an immediate change in climate, terrain and agriculture. Orchards start appearing and apple warehouses become abundant. The city calls itself "The Apple Capital of the World" and its tourist brochure claims "60 percent of the apples sold in the world are from Washington State." I don't object to some enthusiastic backpatting by local tourism, but this is extreme. China produces the bulk of the world's apples and the United States only about 8 percent. Of these, Washington supplies half.

South of Highway 97 the Columbia River divides the city of Wenatchee into Wenatchee and East Wenatchee, the former by far the larger. The name of the city is a Native word meaning "where the waters meet," referring to the confluence of the Columbia and the Wenatchee rivers. Wenatchee is brightened up by a collection of 60 sculptures in public places. These are not grandiose larger-than-life pieces that jump out at visitors; they're smaller works, mounted on pedestals, most of them excellent and skilfully done. Wenatchee makes good use of its riverside with some inviting public spaces.

Attractions

Apple Capital Trail Loop
An 18-kilometre (11-mile) paved loop for hiking and biking runs on the western and eastern sides of the Columbia River and makes use of the two river crossings. The trail is lit until midnight on the west side.

Art on the Avenues
>>> Sculptures enhance the streets of Wenatchee.

The outdoor sculpture gallery, started in 1995, has grown to 60 pieces with some mounted on local columnar basalt. Start downtown or get a map and brochure from the tourist info office for a self-guided sculpture tour.

Bridge of Friendship Japanese Garden
• East Wenatchee
• corner of 9th Street and E. Wenatchee

This public garden serves as a symbol of friendship with sister city Misawa, Japan, which was the starting point for the first non-stop airplane flight across the Pacific Ocean. Two pilots, daredevil stunt flyer Clyde Pangborn and playboy Hugh Herndon, Jr., made the flight in 1931 in a single-engine Bellanca Skyrocket. Their adventure started with a stint in a Japanese prison for flying without permission. Then, overloaded with 3,500 litres (915 gallons) of fuel, they had a long, lumbering takeoff.

Once airborne they suffered a temporary loss of engine power and jettisoned their heavy landing gear by climbing outside the plane to unhook it. Eventually, they landed on a skid plate. Wenatchee became the touchdown location when the plane went off course because the navigator had been daydreaming and other airports were fogged in.

Ohme Gardens

- 3327 Ohme Road
- 509-662-5785

Perched high on a rock bluff overlooking the Wenatchee Valley, Ohme Gardens represents 60 years of work by the Ohme family. Their efforts have transformed a barren, arid hill into lush gardens. The gardens are planted in terraces so that touring them is like taking a short hike. Ponds and lagoons are hidden in coves and around corners.

Wenatchee River

The local waterway is well used for a variety of sports. It is a favourite whitewater destination in the spring. Later in the year, when the flow of water lessens, it becomes a great place for family tubing.

Wenatchee Valley Museum and Cultural Center

- 127 S. Mission Street
- 509-664-3340

Learn about the first non-stop flight across the Pacific as well as the apple industry history and local anthropology. The large museum, located in two former federal buildings downtown, has a store, rental hall, research library and several storeys of exhibits.

Events

Apple Blossom Festival

- East Wenatchee
- last weekend of April through first weekend of May

Run annually since 1919, this is the oldest major festival in Washington. A classic car show and parade occur on the first Saturday in May.

Farmers' Market

- Riverfront Park at the bottom of 5th Street
- Wednesday and Saturday from 8 a.m. to 1 p.m.

Washington State Apple Harvest Festival

- Centennial Park and Convention Center
- late September

Highlights are an apple-bin race, apple-dessert contest and apple-pie-eating contest. A horse-drawn wagon goes up the avenue to children's activities in Centennial Park, while music and beer sales occupy the Convention Center Plaza.

Tourist Info

- 25 N. Wenatchee Avenue, Suite C-111
- 800-572-7753
- www.wenatcheevalley.org

On the Road to Okanogan

You are now travelling on the first portion of US 97 that was added to the state highway system, way back in 1897, when there was hardly a car to be seen. The road started in Wenatchee and went north to Pateros. The highway reached Okanogan in 1905 and extended to the US–Canada border in 1907.

For the next 110 kilometres (70 miles) you travel beside the Columbia River with 97 on the east side and Alt. 97 following along on the west bank. Alt. 97 leads to the vacation town of Chelan, on Lake Chelan, which is in one of the deepest gorges in North America.

>>> Bighorn sheep feed on a reserve north of Wenatchee.

<<< This turbine is on display at the roadside rest stop at Wells Dam.

The average lake width is about 3 kilometres (2 miles) while this lake extends 90 kilometres (55 miles) into the heart of the Cascade Mountains, where peaks exceed 3,000 metres (9,000 feet). A trip up the lake on the year-round ferry, *Lady of the Lake*, connects the arid, desert-like climate of the lower Lake Chelan Valley to fjord-like gorges carved by glaciation. After Chelan, 97 and Alt. 97 merge and keep to the west riverbank.

The next point of interest is Wells Dam on the Columbia River. Completed in 1967, this concrete gravity hydroelectric dam is 1,400 metres (4,460 feet) long and has fish ladders at either end. The Wells Fish Hatchery releases 3 million juvenile salmon and steelhead annually. The grounds provide a pleasant picnic area and a huge out-of-service turbine is displayed.

 PATEROS >>> *population: 650*

Relocated after the Wells dam was built, the town is at the junction of the Methow and Columbia rivers, where the latter widens and becomes Pateros Lake. Pateros was a stopping point for early steamboats that delivered passengers and freight to Okanogan County.

Events
Apple Pie Jamboree

- various locations
- mid July

This event has been going strong for six decades and includes pie eating, baking, throwing and just about anything else you can do with an apple pie. There are also athletic contests, shows, bingo, a chess tournament and other competitions during the three-day event.

BREWSTER >>> *population: 2,200*

At Brewster a sign welcomes you to Okanogan Country and for the next 480 kilometres (300 miles) that is where you will be. In 1811, David Stewart of the Pacific Fur Company established a post here. He was the first White man to travel north and explore the Canadian Okanagan while looking for furs. Near Brewster the Okanogan River vanishes into the mighty Columbia like a garden hose into the ocean.

A trip to Brewster gives you a little bit of Mexico in a northern US state. It's far less expensive than a vacation in Acapulco or the Yucatan, and the culture, on the surface, seems much the same. The town is 60 percent Hispanic, with 9 out of 10 of those people originally from Mexico, many of them migrant farm workers—Washington State is the second largest agricultural producer in the United States.

Pastel-coloured, one-storey concrete buildings are the standard and signs for businesses are in a mixture of English and Spanish. The thing to do in Brewster is to enjoy its Latin flavour, take a dip in the cold Columbia if you can bear it, eat some Mexican food and read the historical signs.

Attractions
Fort Okanogan State Park
- 6.5 kilometres (4 miles) north on 97, then east on Hwy. 17
- 509-923-2473

The fort is gone, but the park includes an interpretive centre that provides information and displays on one of the first settlements in Washington. The fur-trapping history of the area is also explained.

Tourist Info
Chamber of Commerce
- 109 S. Bridge Street
- 509-689-0189

DETOUR >>> **BREWSTER TO THE BORDER**

For those fortunate travellers who frequent this portion of 97, this side trip provides an alternate, albeit lengthier, route between Brewster and the Canada–US border west of Osoyoos.

Just northeast of Brewster, turn left off 97 onto the Old Okanogan Highway into the orchards that lie just above the valley. The rolling countryside features picturesque farms and ranches. On your right is a large group of radio telescopes marked with a sign that reads "Verestar." Unlike the telescopes at the Dominion Radio Astrophysical Observatory in Oliver, B.C., Verestar is under lock and key and, instead of a self-guided tour, it has a No Trespassing sign.

The Old Okanogan Highway becomes #215. Turn left at a sign for Conconully. Here you are in hunting and fishing territory where lodges and camps line the various lakes and rivers. In Conconully turn right at the main intersection (there's only one) and follow the sign that says "Loomis, 23 miles." Buy gas at the only pump if you need it; you won't see any pumps for a while. The pavement becomes washboard dirt, wide enough for a car and a half, and stays that way for close to 20 kilometres (12 miles) as it hugs a small, steep canyon. Nearby Okanogan National Forest is the perfect place for a canoe or kayak paddle or the simple enjoyment of the serene rivers and lakes.

Pavement returns as you reach Loomis, little more than a cluster of houses. Drive through Loomis to Palmer Lake, which is your reward for the rough ride. A turquoise gem at the foot of mountains, the lake is warm and inviting in the summer with sandy beaches at either end. The settlement of Nighthawk is billed as a ghost town but it disappoints. There are some abandoned buildings, but they don't look especially old. Molson (see Oroville), on the other side of Highway 97, is a better bet.

A short way ahead is the tiny Canada–US customs post, open from 9 a.m. to 5 p.m. After passing this outpost, a right turn leads to the town of Osoyoos and a return to Highway 97.

 CONCONULLY >>> *population: 200*

In the 1880s boom time of mining and fur trade, the population of this village approached 5,000 but it has since dwindled to a small dot on a big map. The name comes from the Native word for the surrounding valley, meaning "money hole," for the abundance of beaver.

Conconully hosts two events that are somewhat out of the ordinary. One tests Fear Factor taste buds and the other challenges the ability to push a privy down a snow-covered street. All this (and more) in a community of fewer than 200 characters.

Events
Cowboy Caviar Fete
• mid-June

Also known as the Testicle Festival, this culinary gathering pits restaurants against each other to serve up the bull's dangling participles. The winner gets the Balls to the Wall plaque.

Outhouse Races
• mid-January

If cowboy caviar isn't bizarre enough, then how about winter outhouse races? Two pushers and one rider direct a wooden outhouse along a snowy course through the middle of town. The privy push has been going on for more than two decades.

Tourist Info
Chamber of Commerce
• 509-826-9050, 877-826-9050

On the Road to Gold and Ghosts

Just north of Brewster on the east side of 97, a sign points to a scenic lookout. An unlikely dirt road wanders beside an orchard and takes you to the overlook, a view of the confluence of the Okanogan and Columbia rivers. The slow-moving Okanogan will rise only 30 metres (100 feet) between here and its source at Osoyoos Lake near the international border. Originally, 97 followed the west side of this river, but in the 1950s the highways department shifted the road to the east side.

As you wind northward you pass through a series of small, old-fashioned towns. This is an area of declining population, although it is definitely a pleasant place to live, with lakes, a nice climate, rolling countryside and a river flowing past. The total number of people living in Okanogan County, which runs from Brewster to the border (and just as far east and west), is a mere 25,000.

 **OKANOGAN** >>> *population: 2,400*

This quiet town is the county seat and shares its name with the region and the county.

Attractions
Okanogan County Historical Museum and Fire Hall Museum
- 1410 2nd Avenue N.
- 509-422-4272

Dioramas, models, photographs and exhibits pertaining to local history are displayed, along with a replica of an Old West town of the early 1900s. Outdoor displays include farm equipment and what is believed to be the Okanogan's oldest structure, a log cabin built in 1879. Go back in time through the photography of Frank Matsura, who came to the Okanogan in 1890. The museum is adjacent to Legion Park.

County Courthouse
- junction of Highways 20 and 97

The majestic three-storey courthouse, built in the California Mission Revival style, has looked down on the town from a hillside since it was built in 1915.

Tourist Info
Okanogan Chamber of Commerce
- 509-422-3658

 OMAK >>> *population: 4,700*

Omak's name comes from the Native word for "good medicine," which is often needed during the town's most famous event. Omak is best known for the Omak Stampede, and the Stampede is best known for the controversial Suicide Race, which has been held on the second weekend of August for more than 70 years.

The Stampede includes a rodeo, carnival, parade and powwow. The Suicide Race involves a horde of horses and riders racing down a dirt cliff. Chances are some of them will literally bite the dust, but the landing is usually soft—on the sandy banks, or in the river. The event is held at the Omak Stampede Grounds.

Tourist Info
Omak Chamber of Commerce
- 401 Omak Avenue
- 509-826-4218, 800-225-6625

 TONASKET >>> *population: 1,000*

The area was originally a Native encampment and was named after Chief Tonasket. Recreational activities such as photography and art are promoted while traditional outdoor pastimes such as hunting, fishing and camping take advantage of the natural setting.

Events
Farmers' Market
- Tonasket Triangle Park
- Thursdays, 3 to 6 p.m.

North Country Car Show
- Tonasket Rodeo Grounds
- fourth weekend of June
- 509-486-1222

Antique cars from the valley and beyond are displayed, and there is a drag race for old, slow cars.

Okanogan River Garlic Festival
- History Park on Locust Avenue
- late August

The land surrounding the Okanogan River provides the right combination of climate and soil to make a premier area for growing superior garlic. Everything related to garlic is displayed, plus music, ethnic dance, home baking, produce and workshops. Visitors are challenged to tell the difference between garlic types. Bring breath mints.

Tourist Info
Tonasket Chamber of Commerce
- 866-440-8828, 509-486-4543
- www.tonasketcity.org

Seat of the Crime

While today the Okanogan looks peaceful and rustic there was a time when it bustled with the commerce and crime that exemplified the Wild West. Violence occurred in the many silver mines and their attached communities that pocked the hillsides. Cheap whiskey, prostitution and frequent gun play were common. "The biggest liars and thieves I have ever met," wrote a traveller in 1889, "are honorable, high-minded citizens compared to the beauts who live around here."

In 1888 the first county seat of Okanogan County was established at the mining town of Ruby City. Seven months later voters, disgusted with the lawlessness, moved the county offices to Salmon City, now Conconully. In 1914 the county seat again moved, this time to the town of Okanogan. ♦

 **OROVILLE** >>> *population: 1,600*

Gold was found in the Similkameen River in the 1860s, creating a mini gold rush, so it stands to reason that this town would derive its name from oro, the Spanish word for gold. North of town a historical marker beside 97 tells the story of Hiram F. "Okanogan" Smith, who in the late 1850s became the first White settler in the Okanogan. Smith ran a trading post and later planted over 1,000 apple trees that were carried in by snowshoe and packhorse from Hope, B.C. Eleven of his trees on the east side of the lake are said to still bear fruit.

Attractions
McDonald Cabin
• 915 14th Street

Built in 1882 as a home for the McDonald family, this small cabin became one of the first US customs offices in the area. Customs and pioneer displays can be found inside.

Old Train Depot Museum
• Janis-Oroville Road
• 509-476-2570

The Great Northern Depot began serving Oroville in 1907. Part of the museum is devoted to railroad items and local history, while outside is a Great Northern caboose that was retired in 1987.

Pacific Northwest Trail

This 1,800-kilometre (1,100-mile) wilderness hiking path passes through Oroville as it connects Glacier National Park in Montana to Cape Alava on the Pacific Ocean. Hiking, horseback riding and, for most of the way, biking are all permitted.

Tourist Info
Oroville Chamber of Commerce and Visitor Center
• 1730 Main Street
• 509-476-2739

MOLSON GHOST TOWN

Molson is a ghost-town lover's dream come true: dilapidated wooden buildings to root through, old machinery rusting in the rain, faded

>>> The abandoned buildings of Molson are paradise for historians.

pictures hanging on cracked walls and enough signs and other clues to enable a visitor to put together a picture of a town that might have been. The only missing ingredients are tumbleweed, tall cacti and the bleached skulls of cattle that couldn't find water.

It's accessible by paved road, just 15 minutes from Oroville. The entry sign reads, "Elevation 3,741 ft., population 35." The population is that of Molson's "New Town." The population of the original Molson is zero. The number of residents has declined somewhat from the high of 700 in 1927 when the town had two theatres, five churches, several pool halls, a number of beauty salons, a three-storey brick school, car dealerships and a train station serviced by one freight and two passenger trains every day.

A half-dozen weathered, wooden buildings huddle together on a wide patch of weedy dirt. A cracked sign proclaims nothing more than "Old Molson." No security guards stop you from touching and feeling and no turnstiles seek an admission charge. A bank, two homes, an assay office, a saloon and a tiny building with a barely readable sign, "Knob Hill Exchange," have open doors that welcome wanderers.

In its heyday, Molson was so prosperous that two rival forces vied for power and the New Molson was established to compete with the original. Strategically located between Old and New is the high school, which is now a huge museum (no admission fee—just a subtle request for a donation), and the former mercantile store. The town has many Canadian ties, the strongest being to the Molson family of

Montreal. John Molson, son of the founder of the Molson brewery, was something of a black sheep in the family and was given a weekly stipend to keep his nose out of the family business. As a remittance man he travelled west, ended up in the hills above Okanogan and started a town that he named after himself. As luck would have it, gold was discovered and the town prospered until 1926, when the vein ran out and both Old and New were abandoned.

The high school–museum houses a collection of abandoned household items, such as radios, toasters, stoves, butter makers and dishes. It also has a recreated classroom, an authentic Molson barbershop and an original post office.

To get to Molson turn east on Center Street in Oroville. Turn left on Cherry, then right on Chesaw Road. Turn left where a sign points to Molson. To return by a different route, take the road you came into Molson on past the lake, and continue onto the gravel that runs atop the old rail bed. Eventually this gravel road meets the paved road from Oroville, where you turn right.

On the Road to the Border

Osoyoos Lake straddles the 49th parallel that marks the Canada–US border, and Oroville residents get to take advantage of the clear, warm water flowing from British Columbia's Okanagan. Warm water from the north? Strange but true. So far the source of much of the water along Highway 97—except for the Okanogan River—has been the mountain streams that flow quickly from snow melting at higher altitudes. The water from the Canadian side moves very slowly through a system of seven lakes, several rivers and a number of canals. The low-altitude valley gets plenty of summer sun, the lakes do not freeze in the winter and, as the water travels through the system, it gets plenty of opportunity to warm.

Osoyoos Lake State Park sits at the spot where these waters, for the last time, revert into a river. The Okanogan River forms no more lakes on its journey from here, south to the Columbia River. Continuing along, the next stop is the border. New buildings and more auto and truck lanes have relieved most of the congestion, however late afternoons on summer weekends can still see long lines.

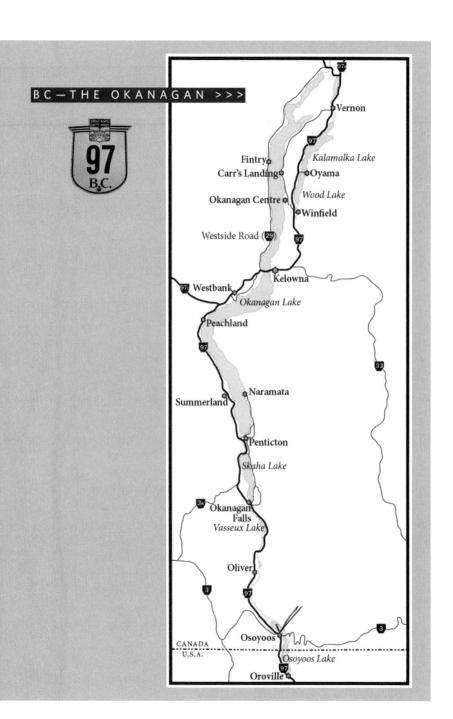

 # British Columbia: The Okanagan

On the Road to Osoyoos

AFTER CROSSING THE BORDER INTO CANADA, YOU IMMEDIATELY NOTICE A change in the countryside. Vineyards and orchards appear everywhere, the valley widens and, with a few exceptions, will continue to widen as it spreads northward. With slightly more rainfall and more irrigation, the terrain resembles Nevada and Arizona less now, although the Osoyoos region is still far from being a rainforest.

The Okanagan/Okanogan is one of the few places along the lengthy Canada–US border where the Canadian side is markedly more populous and prosperous than its US counterpart. While the American countryside is serene and natural, with light automobile traffic and few bicycles and pedestrians, the Canadian countryside is positively bustling. In a reversal of fortunes, gigantic homes and strip malls in the north replace dilapidated houses (some with attached junkyards) in the south. The dusty Okanogan towns with their diminishing populations contrast with thriving Okanagan cities. One possible explanation is that the United States, with its huge range of climates, offers a myriad of retirement locales. In Canada, relatively pleasant winter weather is found only in the Okanagan and on the west coast.

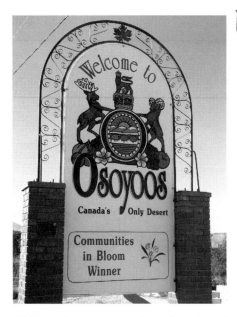

>>> Osoyoos is proud of its desert landscape.

OSOYOOS >> *population: 4,900*

Although there are many ways of calculating mean and average temperatures, Osoyoos has the distinction of generally being considered the warmest city in Canada. The average high in July is about 30°C (86°F), with 249.8 millimetres (10 inches) of annual rainfall: extremely hot and dry by Canadian standards, but cool and moist compared to the desert standards of the American southwest.

One of the unique features of the Osoyoos area is that it sits in Canada's only true desert. The Sonoran (or Sonora, or Great Basin) Desert edges up from Mexico in the rain shadow of the mountains and juts into the southern Okanagan. Known locally as the Pocket Desert, it hosts an abundance of plant and animal life. Small, prickly cacti hug the ground to keep warm, and greasewood, bunchgrass, scorpions and western rattlesnakes make the desert their home.

The town was originally called Soyoos, an Okanagan Native word that means "the narrows" or "the place where two lakes come together." A small bridge now crosses this narrows. Legend has it that Judge Valentine Carmichael Haynes, the first White person born in Soyoos, added the initial "O" to the name to make it sound Irish.

The Osoyoos Indian band of the Okanagan tribe has done some impressive development on some of its desert holdings including a year-round campground (Nk'Mip Resort), a winery and a desert heritage centre. A hotel and second golf course are in the works.

Attractions
Anarchist Mountain

• Highway 3 east

Travelling east on Highway 3 will bring you a couple of the best and most accessible viewpoints in the entire Okanagan. The road winds out of the valley and climbs to mountainside panoramas that encompass lake, town, vineyards and northern Washington. Two parking spots at 9.2 kilometres (5.7 miles) and 10.2 kilometres (6.3 miles) offer the best views. Both stops are among the most photographed spots on the B.C. highway system.

At an elevation of 1,253 metres (4,045 feet), the summit is 20 kilometres (12 miles)

<<< Sunset strollers enjoy Pioneer Walkway.

from town, rising from 277 metres (910 feet) at lake level. The origin of the mountain's name has provoked many stories, including one about a gang of anarchists hiding out there.

Osoyoos is in the odd position of having two interpretive centres that explain desert life, each within a few minutes of the other. Although both have indoor displays and descriptive walks through the sparse terrain, they are different enough that both can be enjoyed without much repetition.

Nk'Mip Desert and Heritage Centre
- Rancher Creek Road
- 250-495-7901, 888-495-8555

This centre, run by the Okanagan Indian band, focuses on Native life and customs and has several First Nations' dwellings located alongside its 2 kilometres (1.2 miles) of gravel trails. Displays highlight Native crafts, customs and foods. The western rattlesnake can sometimes be seen basking in the summer sun. The centre has a program to study the rattlers, which reach a length of 1.5 metres (almost 5 feet). Naturalists have implanted transmitters under the skin of the snakes so they can be tracked. The Snake Hotel is a good place to safely view the slitherers.

Desert Centre
- 146th Avenue off Highway 97
- 250-495-2470, 877-899-0897

The natural desert environment is the focus of this 25-hectare (66-acre) plot of nearly original terrain. The local desert is home to 100 rare plants, 300 rare invertebrates and 30 to 50 percent of Canada's endangered and vulnerable vertebrates. No need to feel overwhelmed by the statistics: a guide conducts tours with stops at information kiosks strategically spaced to give rest and shade and to steer you to rare, unusual or overlooked plants and animals.

Osoyoos Desert Model Railroad

- Buena Vista Industrial Park
- 11611-115 Street
- 250-495-6842

>>> The proprietor pops out of a display at Osoyoos Desert Model Railroad.

The largest Marklin model train layout in North America covers a square footage equal to that of a large home. More than 500 miniature houses and 4,000 hand-painted little people complement a dozen computer-controlled trains that run on a kilometre of HO scale track. This Osoyoos attraction opened in late 2003.

Osoyoos Museum

- bottom of Main Street, next to the lake

Promoted as "the best small town museum in Canada," the main feature is a fine display from the archives of the B.C. Provincial Police. Information is provided about the establishment of local boundaries, the Canada–US border and customs posts. A log cabin from 1879 has been moved to the museum and is on display along with an old liquor distilling apparatus.

Spotted Lake

- south side of Highway 3, 8.3 kilometres (5.1 miles) west of Highway 97

The small lake gets its name from aquamarine circles that dot its surface.

These are concentrations of magnesium sulphate (Epsom salts), calcium, sodium sulphates and other minerals. In the hot sun the water evaporates, crystallizing the minerals and forming white-rimmed circles. It has often been described as "the only one of its kind in North America" and it is said that there is one circle on Spotted Lake for every

<<< Spotted Lake's rings are made of minerals.

day of the year. The Osoyoos Indian band owns the 15-hectare (38-acre) property and the lake is presently separated from the road by a sagging wire fence. Definitely worth stopping to have a look, but not a swim. The lake is in a small valley next to the road and not that easy to spot on a drive-by.

Events
Aboriginal Day

- Nk'Mip Desert Centre
- June 21
- 250-495-7279

On Aboriginal Day powwows, buffalo burger barbecues, salmon bakes, dancing, craft displays, stories, music and other events are presented at First Nations centres here and in other locations along British Columbia's Highway 97. For example, in Penticton the celebrations take place at Okanagan Lake Park, in Kelowna at Ki-Low-Na Friendship Society, in Vernon at the Friendship Centre, in Salmon Arm at the Switsemalph Learning Centre, in Quesnel at LeBourdais Park and in Prince George at Fort George Park. Check locally. At the Osoyoos powwow at Nk'Mip Resort, Native dancers and drummers from across North America entertain and compete for prizes.

Nk'Mip Salmon Bake Festival

- Nk'Mip Resort Community Hall
- end of September

Fresh salmon is baked over an open pit while Natives entertain with traditional songs and dances. Locally brewed beers and wines are available and there is a silent auction.

Wine Festivals
• spring (early May) and fall (early October)
• see Kelowna

Tourist Info
Osoyoos Chamber of Commerce
• Junction of highways 3 and 97
• 250-495-7142
• www.osoyooschamber.bc.ca

On the Road to Oliver

Despite being in the picturesque Okanagan, the short drive from Osoyoos to Oliver is the only local leg that is not particularly scenic or interesting. It can be improved by turning right (while heading north) at Road 22, just north of Osoyoos. This wine route is described ahead (see Oliver Detour) with downtown Oliver as the starting point, but it can be done in reverse.

 OLIVER >>> *population: 4,505*

Oliver is a relatively late settlement, even for the B.C. Interior. Although there had been some gold-rush activity in the surrounding area in the 1880s, it wasn't until 1921 that B.C. premier "Honest" John Oliver began the community as a resettlement area for First World War veterans.

Fur traders were the first outsiders to visit the Oliver area but it was the lure of gold that brought settlers. East of Oliver the settlement of Camp McKinney at one time boasted five hotels and even more saloons. McKinney was abandoned when better-quality gold was found west of Oliver, and the town of Fairview grew to include a school, bank and government offices. In 1902 the lavish Fairview Hotel burned to the ground and shortly thereafter the gold ran out. Today Fairview is nothing more than a weedy field and descriptive sign just a few kilometres along Fairview Road, off Highway 97 south of town. Between Fairview and McKinney is Oliver.

After Premier Oliver began resettlement, an irrigation system was built and the desert became a lush and prosperous fruit-growing area. One of the more interesting local buildings is the Oliver Hotel, which was originally built near Vancouver in 1912. Nine years later it was dismantled and hauled to Penticton by rail, down Skaha Lake by barge and then to Oliver by truck, where it was rebuilt in its present downtown location.

With a dozen wineries within a dozen kilometres (8 miles) of town, Oliver promotes itself as the "Wine Capital of Canada." Local entrepreneurs have transformed the old downtown firehall into the Wine Country Welcome Centre, complete with a tapas-style restaurant, wine and gourmet food boutique, a tour and information centre and a hint of a wine museum.

Oliver's warm, dry climate has attracted a growing contingent of retirees and RVers who have chosen to park their recreational vehicles there year-round rather than continue to make the long, southward snowbird trek each winter. Nine holes of the Inkameep Desert Canyon golf course remain open all winter for the diehards, who usually only miss a few rounds on account of the snow. With the January highs just above freezing, this winter golf is definitely not a shorts and T-shirt affair.

 DETOUR >>> **BLACK SAGE CIRCLE TOUR**

Black Sage Road, which meanders through orchards and vineyards and passes a half dozen picturesque wineries, is a pleasant alternative to Highway 97. From downtown Oliver follow the signs to the hospital and turn right (south) onto Black Sage Road opposite the Osoyoos Indian Band store/office/gas station. You will pass several interesting wineries, the last of which is Burrowing Owl. After that, Black Sage Road becomes Road 22 and passes the photogenic abandoned buildings of the Haynes Ranch before it curves west, crosses the Okanagan River and leads back to Highway 97. Turn right to return to Oliver.

Attractions
Dominion Radio Astrophysical Observatory (DRAO)
- White Lake Road
- 250-493-7505

Looking like oversized satellite dishes, the radio telescopes of the DRAO collect natural radio signals from space. They can "see" through

>>> Radio signals from space get collected at DRAO, near Oliver.

the space dust that blocks the view of ordinary telescopes and pick up signals that tell astronomers more about the components that make up the universe. The eight antennae are situated within a circle of mountains that keeps out man-made radio interference. An informative self-guided tape tour and a small display room make for a pleasant and educational stop. Be prepared to walk in the 500 metres (550 yards) from the road to the facility; car ignitions interfere with the radio reception.

Driving north from Oliver on Highway 97 turn left onto Secrest Road, then right onto Willowbrook Road and left onto White Lake Road. If all goes well you will spot the seven white synthesis telescopes and the big 26-metre telescope in the distance. Unfortunately there are three different White Lake Roads to get lost on and signage to the facility is non-existent. Ask everyone you see for directions. People in this area are very friendly.

Riverside Hiking and Biking

Oliver's riverside ride rates among the best of the family cycling routes along Highway 97. The mostly paved path, which runs beside the Okanagan River, is known formally as the International Bicycling and Hiking Society Trail. It runs from where 97 crosses the Okanagan River, about 5 kilometres (3 miles) north of Oliver, and follows the river for 18.5 kilometres (11 miles), going through Oliver and passing close to several wineries. It will eventually be extended north to Penticton.

Okanagan Gleaners

- 336 Avenue (#3 Road)
- 250-498-8859

Were it not for the Gleaners, tons of perfectly good fruit and vegetables would end up in the dump. In south Oliver, industrious volunteers, including tourists, gather culls and imperfects such as ill-proportioned peppers, soft tomatoes, blemished apples and peas from popped pods. The vegetables are sliced, dehydrated and made into a dried soup mix that is shipped in barrels to underprivileged countries, providing several million cups of soup per year. Vacationers with a day or an hour to spare can help out any morning from May to November.

<<< The Oliver Gleaners turn imperfect fruits and veggies into delicious soups for impoverished countries.

Oliver and District Museum

- 9728 356th Avenue

The Oliver Museum is housed in what was the original 1925 Provincial Police building, which later became Oliver's first heritage building. Relics from Oliver's past are displayed with an emphasis on agriculture. Should you visit the site of the Fairview gold-rush town and wonder what happened to the buildings, you can find part of the answer on the museum grounds where the 1896 Fairview jail rests. Tours are self-guided.

Tinhorn Creek Vineyards

- 32830 Tinhorn Creek Road
- 250-498-3743, 888-484-6467

If only one winery is on your Oliver itinerary this is a good choice. A self-guided tour allows you to spend as much or as little time as you desire viewing the winemaking process. A demonstration vineyard is set up adjacent to the main building. Signs explain planting techniques, disease, harvesting and, most interestingly, the cost of starting a vineyard.

Events
See Meadowlark Festival, Penticton

Kinsmen Pro Rodeo
• Oliver Rodeo Grounds
• last weekend in August
Sanctioned by the Canadian Professional Rodeo Association, this small-town event is very much a traditional rodeo.

Tomato Festival
• Covert Farm
• first weekend in September
• 250-498-2731
If cavorting with ripe tomatoes is your idea of fun, this festival is a must. You can play tomato minigolf or tomato bocce, join in a tug-of-war that lands the losers in a pile of overripe tomatoes or, for the brave, get into the tomato fight, the highlight of the event. Watching is also fun.

Tourist Info
Oliver and District Travel
• Old Train Station
• 36205 93rd Street
• 250-498-6321

 OKANAGAN FALLS >>> *population: 2,000*
The two waterfalls at Okanagan Falls have been replaced by flood-control dams that contain the movement of water between Skaha Lake and the Okanagan River. Skaha is a First Nation's word for dog, and Dogtown, as it was originally known, was a trading and salmon fishing centre for the Native peoples of the region. By the 1890s, Okanagan Falls was being promoted as a settler's paradise in eastern

Canada and is now known for its antiques and summer markets in tents that line the highway.

Attractions

Bassett Heritage House, Museum and Thrift Shop

• Main Street

These three may seem like an odd combination, but there they are, on the right side of Main Street (Highway 97), as you enter town from the south. The little grey Bassett House that houses the museum was ordered from the T. Eaton and Company catalogue in 1909 by the pioneering Bassett family. Arriving in prefabricated kit form at Okanagan Lake by rail, the house crossed the lake on a sternwheeler and was carried the rest of the way to Okanagan Falls by horse-drawn wagon. The thrift shop is in a half-log cabin.

<<< Bassett House was ordered from a catalogue.

Okanagan Falls Trestle

The trestle was reconstructed in 2000 to connect Okanagan Falls to the old Kettle Valley Railway bed across Skaha Lake. The rail trail winds along Skaha on the way to Penticton. Access and parking near Lion's Park.

Tickleberry's and Wurley's

• 1207 Main Street

Located in the same building, the ice cream shop and the fudge maker are something of an OK Falls landmark for the sweet-tooth crowd.

Tickleberry's boasts the "best ice cream in the valley" and with 265 flavours, it's a sure thing that you won't stop at one scoop. Wurley's Chocolate and Fudge Company whips up 80 varieties of fudge and almost as many types of chocolate in big vats on the premises.

On the Road to Super Scenery

Tighten your seat belts, roll down the windows, get out the camera, focus the binoculars, throw away the map and wander along the waterways. For the next 160 kilometres (100 miles) you will experience some of the greatest scenery and driving pleasure on this continent. Excuse my bias, but I have driven this section of Highway 97 hundreds of times and I have yet to stop gawking. Sailboats cut a white path through bright blue waters at the foot of mountains while the scent of fruit blossoms caresses the nose. The road dips to the lakeshore, perfect for a swim or picnic, and then rises to hilltops for panoramic vistas.

North from downtown Okanagan Falls, Highway 97 follows the west side of Skaha Lake and leads to Penticton. By ignoring the left turn at Okanagan Falls' only main intersection as you head north, and also by ignoring the signs directing you to 97, you will be led around the east side of the lake. I recommend taking the time to circle around scenic Skaha, so follow 97 to Penticton and read the section entitled "Detour: Circling Skaha."

 PENTICTON >>> *population: 42,500*

Penticton was once known as the Peach City for the prolific fruit-growing in the area. It now uses the motto A Place to Live Forever, which is close to what the word Penticton means in the Interior Salish language. Equally apt is the moniker Beach City, as Penticton is gloriously situated between the south end of Okanagan Lake and the north end of Skaha Lake, with vast stretches of sandy beach along both bodies of water.

Coming into Penticton on 97 offers three choices. Follow the signs for 97 and you will turn left and be led alongside a channel, down which rafters and tubers float in the summer, and then out of town. This is the least interesting choice. Stay off 97 for the option of going into downtown Penticton (well signed) and seeing more of this pretty city. Heading towards downtown and then taking a brief jog east on

<<< The old Penticton information booth is now a peachy beverage stand.

Yorkton Avenue provides a third option: the circle tour of Skaha Lake.

In the north end of Penticton near the city limits, a small bridge passes over the Okanagan River Channel. This waterway, created by the city founders, eliminated swampland, controlled flooding and made it possible to build the city. Before crossing the channel, turn right (north) until Okanagan Lake makes it impossible to go any farther and then turn left until the channel prevents travel in that direction. Here you will find a 30-year-old rose garden next to a minigolf and bumper boat establishment. Less than a kilometre downstream (south) there is a spot to launch an inflated raft or tube to ride the channel (see "Coyote Cruises").

Attractions
Apex Mountain
• Green Mountain Road
• 250-292-8222

Apex Mountain is primarily a snow-sport resort, but it reopens in early summer for hiking and biking. Walkers and riders take a chairlift to the summit for the best of scenery and effortless descents. Located 33 kilometres (21 miles) west of Penticton, Apex is one of the Okanagan's three major winter resorts.

Art Gallery of the Southern Okanagan
• 199 Front Street
• 250-493-2928

In a pretty setting close to the lake, the gallery features exhibits by local and national artists. Behind the gallery is the new Ikeda Japanese Garden.

Fruit Ripening Times

The sweet smells and buzzing bees of spring-blossom time in the Okanagan are only a prelude to the richness of the fruit harvest. Munching a handful of sun-warmed cherries and spitting the pits out the car window is a blissful summer experience.

Picking times in the Valley differ greatly depending on bloom times, weather and temperature. In a bad year, fruit can ripen much later than usual. Crops ripen earlier in the South Okanagan (Oliver area) than the Central and North Okanagan. The following is a general timetable of when blooms appear and crops are picked in the Valley.

Blossom Times

Cherries, mid- to late April
Apricots, early to mid-April
Peaches, mid-April
Apples, late April to early May
Pears, mid- to late April
Prunes and plums, mid-April
Grapes, late April to mid-May

Harvest Times

Cherries, June 18 to July 15
Apricots, July 8 to August 18
Peaches, July 25 to September 15
Ground Crops, July to mid-September
Apples, August 1 to September 15
Pears, August 10 and onward
Plums, August 12 to September 15
Grapes, August 30 and onward ◆

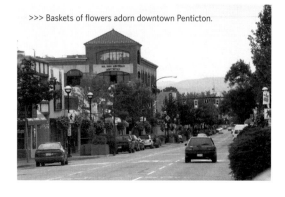

>>> Baskets of flowers adorn downtown Penticton.

Books n' Things

- 238 Main Street
- 250-492-6661

The biggest bookstore on the entire length of Highway 97 has more used books than the owners can count, plus nearly 10,000 videos for rent. The videos represent the owner's esoteric tastes, while the books cover nearly every subject. Best place in B.C. for the bibliophile and videophile.

Coyote Cruises

- 215 Riverside Road
- 250-292-2115

Tube and raft rentals are available to float down the channel to Skaha Lake, and there is a bus to bring you back. You can also launch your own raft here.

Penticton Museum (a.k.a R.N. Atkinson Museum)

- 785 Main Street, attached to the library
- 250-490-2451

The museum has an excellent presentation of pioneer and First Nations' artifacts, wildlife, railways and boating that date back to Penticton's inception. Here is where you can learn about the clearing of the swamp that became the site of Penticton. Dioramas of nature are impressive, as are old train station memorabilia.

S.S. *Sicamous* Heritage Park
- 1099 Lakeshore Drive W.
- 250-492-0403

The S.S. *Sicamous* is the largest remaining steel-hulled sternwheeler in Canada. Along with its sister ship, the S.S. *Naramata*, constructed about the same time, the *Sicamous* sits on the beach at the south end of Okanagan Lake. It is easy to understand why the beautifully fitted, 70-metre (228-foot) sternwheeler attained the regal title, "The Queen of Okanagan Lake."

<<< An hour-long float down the canal is a Penticton summer ritual.

Skaha Bluffs
Slightly south of Penticton and northeast of Skaha Lake lies one of the top-10 rock-climbing spots in North America. Skaha gets its repu-tation not from its height, but from the wide variety and large number of climbs its multiple peaks offer. Additionally it practically guarantees warm sunny weather—not your usual mountain climate. More than 60 different crags and 600 routes can be accessed from the main Loop Trail.

<<< The steamship *Sicamous* has become a museum.

Go south on Main Street, left on Crescent and right onto Valleyview Road to the parking area where a long, steep set of stairs leads to the 8-kilometre (5-mile) Loop Trail.

Queen of Okanagan Lake

From her launch in 1914 until she was retired in 1937, the 310-passenger steel-hulled sternwheeler S.S. *Sicamous* departed Penticton every morning for a 250-kilometre (150-mile) round-trip to Okanagan Landing with as many as 20 stops at isolated communities.

The *Sicamous* ("shimmering water" in the Native language) was fitted out to be anything but a workhorse and was a cut above the usual freshwater passenger boat. Serviced by a crew of 38, her luxurious interior of Australian mahogany and Burmese teak featured 40 staterooms with electric lights and steam heat. A dining room accommodated 70 guests, who were served with silver and fine china by waiters in white jackets and bow ties. Passengers could relax in the smoking or observation room or use the writing desks on one of the ship's balconies.

With a top speed of 19 miles (31 kilometres) per hour, the *Sicamous* must have been a pretty sight churning up the waters of Okanagan Lake. The latest in firefighting equipment, 20 watertight compartments and 6 lifeboats made her safe, if not unsinkable. The restored ship is now a nautical museum and the scene of on-board plays and musical theatre with a historical bent. ◆

Events
Beach Blanket Film Festival
- east of Lakeside Resort
- third weekend in July, three evenings starting at 10 p.m.

A full-size screen floating on Okanagan Lake is the venue for this Canadian film fest. For a dozen years audiences have curled up on blankets under a starry sky and enjoyed the show.

Dragon Boat Festival
- Rotary Park, Okanagan Lake
- early September

The Saturday and Sunday morning races are a prelude to the bigger Kelowna event. The 20 paddlers in each boat race 500 metres (550 yards) parallel to the beach in front of Lakeside Resort.

Fall Harvest Festival, Farmers' Market
- Gyro Park
- mid-September

This extension of the farmers' market celebrates the work of farmers and growers with highland dancing, belly dancing, tai chi sword play, contests, prizes, free draws and demonstrations by the Society for Creative Anachronism. Children build fruit and veggie sculptures.

Farmers' Market
- 100 block of Main Street
- Saturday mornings

For this large market, the season runs from May to October.

Fest of Ale
- Penticton Trade and Convention Centre
- 273 Power Street
- early April weekend
- 250-492-4355

Organizers claim that this is the biggest beer festival in Canada, with more than 25 breweries and microbreweries showcasing about 75 varieties. Most are B.C. brews, but a few come from Washington State and Alberta. In addition to beer drinking, there is food and entertainment. Attendance is usually close to 6,000.

Highland Games

- King's Park
- early July

Events include sports, a pipe band competition, Scottish highland dancing, piobairechd (droning bagpipes), ceilidh and drumming. Tests of strength are tossing of the stone, the hammer, the caber and the sheaf.

Ironman Canada Triathlon

- 225 kilometres of locations
- end of August

Normally athletic contests would not make this listing, but this is the biggest happening of the year for Penticton, involving 1,800 athletes plus coaches, friends and sponsors from 30 countries and 4,500 local volunteers. For more than 20 years the oldest Ironman race in continental North America has featured the largest single-wave swim start (1,800 athletes). Competitors swim 3.8 kilometres (2.4 miles), bike ride 179 kilometres (111 miles) and run 42.4 kilometres (26.75 miles). Anyone who competes is a champion athlete.

Meadowlark Festival

- various locations in the South Okanagan
- six days encompassing May long weekend
- 250-492-5275

Hikes, lectures, garden tours, birdwatching, astronomy, biking, boating, gardening, horseback tours and nature photography are among the 80 offerings of this week-long event. Most are held in rural areas near Osoyoos, Oliver, Okanagan Falls and Penticton.

Peach City Beach Cruise

- Lakeshore Drive
- third week of June
- 866-889-2288

A three-day antique and classic car convention draws crowds of close to 25,000 who come to see the 700-odd restored vehicles lined up along the road next to Okanagan Lake. Although the display of rods, antique and classic cars is the main attraction, an outdoor concert, entertainment, concessions and a dance round out this family-oriented event.

Peachfest
- Gyro Park
- second week of August

Peachfest has been Penticton's premier summer festival for the past 60 years. It features five days of family entertainment such as sandcastle building, concerts, two parades, a pancake breakfast and the crowning of Miss Penticton. Plenty of ripe, juicy peaches just off the trees add to the flavour. Sunday's activities are designed for kids.

Pentastic Hot Jazz Festival
- second weekend of September

Four venues, including the S.S. *Sicamous* paddlewheeler, host performances by jazz and Dixieland bands from all over North America. Lots of dining and dancing, with a shuttle bus travelling between events. Free performance Sunday at Gyro Park.

Square Dance Jamboree
- Convention Centre
- early August

With numerous local dancers and thousands coming from outside for this event, Penticton has been considered the Square Dancing Capital of Canada.

Wine Festivals
- spring (early May) and fall (early October)
- see Kelowna

Tourist Info
Penticton Info Centre
- 888 Westminster Avenue W.
- 250-492-4103, 800-663-5052
- www.penticton.ca

 DETOUR >>> **CIRCLING SKAHA**

Skaha Lake is cradled between Penticton on its north shore and Okanagan Falls to the south. It is not a big lake and it is one of the few in the Okanagan that can be easily circled either by automobile or bicycle. The round trip totals less than 33 kilometres (20 miles). From a scenic point of view the best way to drive around a body of water is clockwise, so that you are in the right lane, with the best view.

Following the road along the east side of Skaha Lake is a pleasant alternative to Highway 97 and there is no significant increase in time or distance. Bike riders are advised that the bike lane on the east side is intermittent and in several places the road is wide enough for two small cars and little else.

From Penticton follow S. Main Street southward; it eventually becomes Skaha Lake Road and your route around the lake. For the complete circle, just keep the water on your right until you get back to where you started. At that point, a slight jog is needed to complete the route.

After 7 kilometres (4 miles) or so watch for a sign indicating a California bighorn sheep habitat. These are the big boys with massive curly horns. They require a specific habitat and this stretch of cliff, hillside and grassland provides a safe retreat. Hiking trails abound and if you search the hillside you might catch sight of the elusive ungulates.

The little town of Okanagan Falls straddles the south end of Skaha Lake. Any of the parks along the lake and the Okanagan River offer a pleasant spot for rest and contemplation before completing the circuit along 97 and back to Penticton.

 NARAMATA >>> *population: 2,000*

Naramata's isolated setting at the end of a road is part of its charm. About 16 kilometres (10 miles) northeast of Penticton, the village is framed by terraced hillsides planted with fruit trees and vineyards. The unincorporated community occupies but 100 or so hectares (250 acres) along the east shore of the Okanagan Lake. Small beaches and picnic spots can be found at either end of the community.

There is no road along the rugged east side of Okanagan Lake to Kelowna, although there have been attempts to build one. As you arrive from Penticton (as is most likely—you can also arrive from Kelowna by way of Chute Lake, on a rough road), one of the first sights you see is Munson Mountain. Mountain is really a bit of a misnomer as you can drive most of the way to the top. The pavement stops before the summit, but the final walk provides awesome vistas of the lake and of Penticton. A footpath here leads to the big white letters, visible from Highway 97, that spell PENTICTON on the hillside.

The village's melodic name may sound a bit Japanese, but legend gives the name ghostly origins. During a seance, town founder John Moore Robinson supposedly heard the spirit of an Aboriginal chief intone his wife's name, Nar-ra-mat-tah.

Attractions

Claybank Farm Lavender

- 610 Boothe Road
- 250-496-5788

Claybank Farm specializes in growing several varieties of lavender on its second-generation farm. Visitors can take self-guided tours through the fragrant fields and learn to make a decorative lavender wand. Best Bloom Days take place the first week in July, followed by the plant harvest. Samples and sales of handcrafted lavender lotions and potions are available.

Naramata Heritage Inn

- 3625 First Street
- 250-496-6809

>>> Over the years the Naramata Heritage Inn has functioned as a hotel, a private girls' school and as the home of its builder's granddaughter.

John Moore Robinson, an energetic gentleman who started several Okanagan towns, initiated the fruit-growing industry in this region. He also built the Naramata Inn in 1908. Over the years the inn has functioned as a hotel, a private girls' school and as the home of Robinson's granddaughter.

The inn was in a sad state when it was purchased, renovated and revitalized in the late 1990s. The new owners tried to duplicate the details and furnishings of the original building as closely as possible and the result is an architectural blast from the past. Private balconies overlook the lake and the grounds.

Naramata Heritage Museum

- Robinson at Second Street
- 250-496-5866

Old photos and artifacts of early Naramata and the surrounding areas are on display in this small museum.

Events
May Day

- Manitou Park
- May 24 weekend

Naramata is one of the few communities in the British Commonwealth to still host the traditional maypole dance. On Victoria Day (May long weekend) the May Queen is crowned and local children dance around the maypole.

Naramata August Faire

- Manitou Park
- first Sunday in August

A day in the park with a family-oriented festival of live music, food, games and artisans. This annual party, which has run for almost 30 years, starts with a parade at 11 a.m. (remember, this is a village of 2,000, so temper expectations). Free admission.

 SUMMERLAND >>> *population: 11,000*

Summerland's town centre was moved from its original location on the shore of Okanagan Lake in 1905. It now sits at a higher elevation 16 kilometres (10 miles) north of Penticton, in the shadow of Giant's Head Mountain.

>>> Highway
97 skirts
Okanagan
Lake, south of
Summerland.

Between 1915 and 1964, Summerland was an important stop on the Kettle Valley Railway. It is another of the rare communities along 97 that does not have the highway as its main street. No one gets lost downtown as it is rectangular with four main streets. Summerland, in addition to several wineries, has two major and a couple of minor tourist attractions. The Kettle Valley Steam Railway and the Ornamental Gardens are the big ones.

Attractions

Giant's Head Mountain

• Giant's Head Road off Rosedale Avenue

This park is named for the face that nature has carved on the side of the mountain. Some application of imagination is required. A new, paved road leads right to the top of the 910-metre (3,000-foot) mountain where lofty views of the lake, the Kettle Valley Railway, Highway 97 and the town await. Helpful signs let you know exactly what you are looking at.

Kettle Valley Steam Railway

• 18404 Bathville Road
• 877-494-8424

The Kettle Valley Railway was designed to complete the Coast-to-Kootenay rail connection between the B.C. Interior and the west coast. Survey work began in 1910 and the completed line, which ran from

<<< A 1924 engine steams along Summerland's Kettle Valley Railway.

Midway to Hope, was opened on September 14, 1916. The KVR made it possible to get fruit to market and ore and lumber to the coast in record time. In 1964 the railway made its final passenger run and most of the track was torn up. The remaining 16-kilometre (10-mile) stretch between Prairie Valley Station and Canyon View Station is still open for business.

Throughout the season, which runs from the long weekend in May until Thanksgiving, passengers on the KVR will encounter train robberies, murder mysteries, live music and passengers in period costumes. The 105-minute trip winds through typical Okanagan landscape and onto the Trout Creek Trestle, the highest railway bridge on the original line. Two different steam engines take turns pulling (and pushing) the passenger cars, a 1924 Shay #3 and a 1912 Consolidation 3716.

Follow the KVR arrows west out of Summerland about 10 kilometres (6 miles) to the Prairie Valley Station. A small museum at the station explains KVR history.

Nixdorf Classic Cars

- 250-494-4111
- 15809 Logie Road

If you ever visited a car dealership in the 1950s or 1960s the memories will flood back as you walk into the Nixdorf lobby with its black-and-white tiled floor, soda fountain and Buddy Holly songs. About 30 vintage cars are in a rotational display from a private collection of 90.

Summerland Museum and Archives

• Wharton Street

Displays, photographs and videos depict the land, pioneers, farming, packing houses, Kettle Valley Railway and the early homes of the Okanagan Valley. The museum is home to a 50-foot mural, an old KVR ticket booth and an HO gauge railway layout that shows the town as it was in 1950.

Summerland Ornamental Gardens

• 4200 Highway 97
• 250-494-6385

When Agriculture Canada laid out the gardens at its experimental agricultural labs south of Summerland in 1916, its purpose was to "smooth the edges" of the rugged Okanagan landscape. Over time a unique 6-hectare (15-acre) garden developed that was popular with the locals and the increasing numbers of tourists.

Today the vast array of trees, flowers and shrubs features a rose garden, rockery, xeriscape (dry) garden, museum, hummingbird visitor centre and a canyon walk to the KVR Trout Creek trestle. Picnic facilities and informative signs add to the pleasure. The Friends of the Research Station Gardens Society is responsible for educating the public and promoting the gardens. Admission is free but donations are encouraged to support the work of the society. The orchards and big greenhouse that you pass on the way in are part of the Pacific Agri-Food Research Centre. Many varieties of Okanagan fruit have been developed here.

The long, climbing drive to the gardens is off Highway 97, opposite Sunoka Beach, 5 kilometres (3 miles) south of Summerland and 9 kilometres (6 miles) north of Penticton.

Summerland Sweets

• 6206 Canyon View Drive
• 800-577-1277

Here, right before your eyes, Okanagan fruit is transformed into jams, jellies, syrups and confections. The large store offers bargains on factory seconds. You can watch a short demonstration video, then enjoy complimentary samples of syrups poured over ice cream.

Summerland Trout Hatchery

- Lakeshore Drive, just off 97
- 250-494-0491

The oldest continuously running trout hatchery in B.C. dates back to 1928. It rears mostly rainbow trout that are stocked in approximately 275 lakes in the B.C. Interior each year. Self-guided tours of the interpretive centre depict the hatchery program and feature aquariums, models, videos and displays.

Events
Action Festival

- Dale Meadows Complex and other locations
- early June weekend

A parade, the Giant's Head Run, Man of Steel Triathlon and slo-pitch tournament are the highlights. The Giant's Head Run on Sunday is a 5- or 10-kilometre race for all ages.

Paddle Festival

- Powell Beach, Summerland
- mid-June weekend
- 250-862-8049

The Okanagan Paddle Festival features races, displays and demos of kayaks, canoes and outriggers. Free admission with a small charge to try out boats.

Tourist Info
Summerland Chamber of Commerce

- 15600 Highway 97
- 250-494-2686

 PEACHLAND >>> *population: 5,000*

Not only was John Moore Robinson able to hear voices at a seance, he also recognized potential when he saw it. After making his fortune in the newspaper business in central Canada, Robinson became president of a company that operated gold mines on the mountainsides above Peachland. He quickly realized that gold could also grow on trees: he was instrumental in the growth of the area's agriculture and in the survey and development of three towns, Peachland, Summerland and Naramata. Peachland was incorporated in 1909.

Road Development in the Okanagan

The first White exploration of the Canadian Okanagan and the American Okanogan valleys took place along the fur-brigade trail that began at Fort Okanogan near present-day Brewster, Washington, where the Okanogan River disappears into the Columbia River. Starting in 1811, traders used this route to travel north for animal trapping and then to carry the furs along the west side of Okanagan Lake back to the Columbia River and access to the ocean and international markets. Use of this trade route slowly diminished as the fur supply became depleted and markets changed. The last horse train went through in 1847.

Despite the lack of an established wagon trail, a nine-wagon convoy from Walla Walla, Washington, made it to Osoyoos and then to Peachland in 1858 by following a route that approximates Highway 97 today. At Peachland they dismantled the wagons, built 50 rafts from logs and floated their supplies across the lake to Mission Creek on the outskirts of Kelowna. The horses and cattle couldn't make the lake crossing so they had to backtrack to the base of the lake at Penticton and then come up the treacherous, mountainous east side to join the others. The 200-kilometre (125-mile) trip was over territory so rugged that a road on the east side of the lake has yet to be completed.

The lengthy and hazardous routes that connected settlements within the Okanagan Valley inspired a petition, in January 1875, to the Provincial Secretary's office in Victoria, requesting a road from the head of Okanagan Lake (the lake's most northerly point) to Kelowna. A contract for $23,000 was awarded to Phillip Parke for a wagon road 5.5 metres wide (18 feet) and 60 kilometres long (38 miles). The road was completed that same year with ditches on each side,

The layout of Peachland is ideal for taking advantage of sun, sand and the warm lake. The village's homes and commercial buildings are on the west side of the main street, while the lake side is public land. Nearly 4 kilometres (2.5 miles) of public lakeshore is dotted with playgrounds, a marina and boat launch, lawns, picnic areas and beaches complete with lifeguards.

Ogopogo, the mythical Okanagan Lake monster, is said to make its home in an underwater cave across the lake from Peachland, between Rattlesnake Island and Squally Point. The Interior Salish people knew Ogopogo as Nihaiaiitk, the lake demon, and its snake-like image appears in several petroglyphs in the Powers Creek area. A few years ago a million-dollar reward was offered for conclusive proof of Ogopogo's existence. No one managed to snap a portrait.

A drive through Peachland is a pleasant deviation from busy Highway 97, adding only a couple minutes of travel time. There are several entry points to the town.

Attractions

Antlers Beach

• beside the lake on 97, 5 kilometres (3 miles) south of town

This lakeside spot has picnic tables and a place to swim. A sign commemorates a wildlife fence completed in 1998 that stretches from Summerland to Peachland alongside the highway. It has prevented many automobile collisions with deer. The sign claims that deer come from as far as 70 kilometres (45 miles) away to winter by the warm lake.

Hardy Falls

• 4 kilometres (2.5 miles) south of town, off 97

Turn west at Antlers Beach recreation area and stop after about 100 metres (330 feet). On a hot summer's day this is the only place in Peachland as good as the beach. A 10-minute walk along Deep Creek on a path that bridges the twisting creek eight times takes you to Hardy Falls. The 10-metre (33-foot) waterfall fills a gorge with cool mist and you can wade on the rocky creek bed below the cataract. Dippers (water ouzels) fly past and roost in the rocks. Namesake Harry Hardy was one of the first orchardists in the area.

Parrot Island Sanctuary

- 5090 MacKinnon Road
- 250-767-9030

Several dozen abandoned, neglected or relinquished parrots have been rescued by Ray and Val Parkes and given new homes. Guided tours and demonstrations are offered. The sanctuary relies on donations to operate.

Peachland 1910 Museum

- south end of town on Beach Avenue

The unusual, eight-sided wooden building is a former Baptist Church that was constructed in 1910. Exhibits, artifacts and photographs depict the history of the town and the district.

Events
Peachland Fall Fair

- Community Centre
- second weekend of September
- 250-767-2218

This is one of the smaller autumn festivals, but it is a prime example of a traditional fall fair based on the display and judging of fruit, vegetables and crafts.

Polar Bear Dip

- on the beach
- New Year's Day
- 250-767-2455

100 metres (330 feet) of corduroy and 11 bridges (each 4.5 metres or 14 feet wide) totalling 175 metres (543 feet) in length. In places it followed the present Highway 97, while in others it took the route of least resistance and meandered over the countryside. Rather than cutting into the steep banks beside Kalamalka Lake south of Vernon as the highway now does, the wagon road went up into the hills and took an indirect route to Vernon. This road was (and still is) called Mission Road as it was the route to Kelowna, originally called Mission because of the Pandosy Mission, the first dwelling in the area.

Between 1863 and 1891 there was a flurry of road building as more people came into the Okanagan and wagon roads were needed to replace the narrow horse trails. Most of these wagon roads eventually became routes for automobiles and were gradually widened to the two or more lanes we drive on today.

In 1909 a new road linking Peachland and Summerland was constructed, but it had to be abandoned due to constant rockslides. A road along the lake to Penticton had similar problems, but was not abandoned.

Nearly 40 years after the original contract to Phillip Parke, a new road, now Highway 97, was built along the lakeshore to shorten the route between Kelowna and Vernon. It was reported in Victoria's *Times Colonist* of November 23, 1913, that "Kelowna, working northward, has constructed 6.5 miles of macadam road (compacted gravel) to connect with Vernon." In the article, the area was called "the Italy of Canada" with "sun, clear skies, roses, petunias, mignonette, honey suckle, sweet peas and carnations." ◆

As many as 65 hardy souls take the cold plunge. Free hot chocolate, certificates and prizes for those brave enough to make it into the waves. Wearing funny costumes is part of the tradition. Bring a bathing suit and towel. Sunblock is optional.

Tourist Info
Peachland Museum
- 5890 Beach Avenue
- 250-767-3441
- www.peachland.ca

On the Road to Westbank and Kelowna

After Peachland, 97 climbs upwards to Westbank, a community that you won't see much of because it is hidden behind a barricade of billboards—the worst disfiguration on all of 97. I recommend making a right turn at the Glen Rosa interchange (a left turn goes to Crystal Mountain ski area) towards Okanagan Lake, a pleasant detour away from the commercial overload.

 DETOUR >>> **LAKESHORE ESCAPE**

Tens of thousands of automobiles zoom through Westbank daily, with their harried drivers on autopilot. But there is a scenic and tranquil alternative. As soon as you descend the hill after turning towards the lake at the Glenrosa interchange, you will come to a beautiful oasis with a small waterfall. The road then follows the creek. To the right, along Whitworth Road, the Gellatly Nut Farm has recently been developed as a historical site.

Curve left at the lake and you are on Gellatly Road, which becomes Boucherie Road, a delightful, 3-kilometre (2-mile) stretch of peaceful lakeside favoured by cyclists and pedestrians. This route can take twice as long as 97 because you will be tempted to stop for a swim, a short walk beside a rolling river or a wine tasting. Wineries on this route are Little Straw, Mount Boucherie, Quails' Gate and Mission Hill.

Near the spot where Powers Creek enters the lake, opposite the boat launch and yacht club, a pleasant nature walk spans the creek over wooden bridges. Next you will pass Gellatly Bay Aquatic Park, Kent Park and Rotary Park. Boucherie Road joins up with 97 about 2.5 kilometres

<<< Westbank artwork "watches" traffic pass on 97.

(1.5 miles) before the bridge to Kelowna. A right turn takes you to Kelowna, but you still have to face the worst section of the billboard blight, on Westbank First Nations' land, before reaching the bridge.

 WESTBANK >>> *population: 36,000*

Attractions

Crystal Mountain Ski Resort

- 12.5 kilometres (8 miles) from 97 along Glenrosa Road
- 250-768-5189

The small (three main lifts) local hill has big plans to become a year-round resort, but likely not before 2010.

Gellatly Nut Farm Park

- Whitworth Road
- 250-707-1042

Canada's first commercial nut orchard has a number of 100-year-old trees plus a 150-metre (485-foot) stretch of lakeshore, a playground and a few heritage buildings. In October and November visitors can collect their own nuts from the ground or buy nuts that are already picked and ready to be bagged, weighed and shelled. Head protection is advised, as the falling nuts can make an impact. Chestnuts, walnuts, heartnuts, filberts (hazelnuts), butternuts and black walnuts are all available.

Mission Hill Family Estate Winery

- 1730 Mission Hill Road
- 250-768-6498, 250-768-6448

Of the hundreds of wineries on and around Highway 97, the most spectacular of them all is situated atop a big hill (or small mountain) overlooking Okanagan Lake and the surrounding area. Mission Hill Family Estate Winery is an architectural wonder built in the style of a Moorish castle, with no expense spared. It features a 12-storey bell tower with four bronze bells handcrafted in Annecy, France, by the Paccard Bell Foundry.

The flowery grounds, planted with 4,000 trees and shrubs, plus the valley vistas, are worth the short trip. A grass amphitheatre occasionally hosts musical and Shakespearian presentations, and the view and ambience alone make any theatrical presentation memorable.

>>> The bronze bells in the spectacular bell tower were handcrafted in France.

Westbank Museum
- 2736 Lower Glenrosa Road
- 250-768-0110

Close to 4,000 pioneer artifacts collected from around the world, many relating to the Westbank area, are exhibited. An extensive rock-and-mineral collection and photographs of Native pictographs are also on view.

Tourist Info
Westbank Chamber of Commerce
- Unit # 4, 2375 Pamela Road
- 250-932-5528

 DETOUR >>> **WESTBANK TO VERNON**

Highway 97 hugs the east side of Okanagan Lake, but the pretty blue waters vanish from sight as soon as you cross the bridge into Kelowna. The highway does, however, follow the shores of three smaller lakes.

This alternative, 90-kilometre (55-mile) route sticks close to the west side of Okanagan Lake, past provincial parks and historic Fintry, before greeting Highway 97 just outside of Vernon. If your destination is Kamloops, this route takes about the same amount of time as 97 and may be quicker if Kelowna traffic is heavy

Heading towards Kelowna on 97 after leaving Westbank, turn left (north) at the traffic lights onto Westside Road (frequently spelled West Side Road). Westside Road soon narrows and becomes a twisting black ribbon of asphalt that curls along the hillside abutting the lake. A moment's inattention and you could be rolling down 50 metres (160 feet) of unguarded cliff. The road is slowly being improved but careful and cautious driving is required. The many viewpoints are superb and worth investigating.

Immediately to the right as you start along Westside Road is Old Ferry Wharf Road. Here the ferry that crossed the lake's narrowest point docked with cars and cargo before the bridge across Okanagan Lake was built.

Bear Creek Provincial Park, a popular campground and a pleasant place to hike, picnic and swim, is about 8 kilometres (5 miles) from the turnoff at 97. The trailhead is across the road from the park and leads to a waterfall on Bear Creek that is impressive in the spring, but becomes a trickle in autumn.

Fintry, or more properly Fintry Delta, is farther north at the mouth of Short's Creek, just off the road. This is recreation with a historical flavour. The village was once the transportation hub of Okanagan Lake: streams of Hudson's Bay Company fur traders passed through here while steamers docked daily on their routes around the lake.

A walking trail leads to waterfalls, the deep pools of Short's Creek, a suspension bridge and the remains of irrigation and power-generation structures. Other features from the past include part of the old ferry wharf, a preserved manor house, a caretaker's house and several barns including a rare octagonal one.

Just beyond Fintry, Westside Road passes through property owned by the Okanagan Indian Band and then it meets Highway 97. A right turn takes you past O'Keefe Ranch to north Vernon and a left has you on the way to Kamloops.

KELOWNA >>> *population: 110,000*

Situated at the narrowest part of Okanagan Lake, Kelowna is the most populous city on the entire length of Highway 97 as well as being the hub of the Okanagan Valley and the largest shopping district between Vancouver and Calgary. Kelowna is also among the oldest communities on 97 and welcomed the first European settlers in the Okanagan Valley. A mission was established near what came to be known as Mission Creek in 1859 by Fathers Charles Pandosy and Pierre Richard, two Oblate Catholic missionaries. Amazingly, four of the original mission buildings still stand and are open to the public.

Kelowna's name has a good story behind it. A prominent White settler who lived in a partly underground shanty was a rather hairy man who the Natives called kemxtus, meaning black bear's face. When it came time to give the settlement an

The Laird of Fintry's Manor House

The Laird of Fintry was Captain James Cameron Dun-Waters, a Scotsman who inherited a fortune at age 22. A passionate sportsman, he travelled the world in pursuit of big game. In 1908 while hunting in the Okanagan he knew he had found his home. Dun-Waters bought his delta on the lake and renamed it "Fintry" after his Scottish home. He sold his estate in Scotland and, with his wife, Alice, and a few servants, developed his personal empire.

Fintry Manor was built between 1910 and 1911 using local brick and granite quarried from a cliff on the property. In 1924, the same year that Dun-Waters's wife died, the manor house was destroyed by fire. He immediately rebuilt it on the same foundations, with improvements that included an octagonal barn for his famous Ayrshire dairy herd.

In his 30 years at Fintry, Dun-Waters developed the delta into a productive farm and impressive estate. He could have lived a life of leisure, but he was a man of action. He held a director-ship in the CPR, played a strong role in the B.C. Fruit Growers Association

>>> Golf courses and the lake are major Kelowna attractions.

official name this was thought to be appropriate, but too difficult, so Kelowna, female grizzly bear, was substituted.

The first landmark that distinguishes Kelowna for visitors driving in from the west is the bridge that spans Okanagan Lake. Because of the soft, deep lake bottom, the bridge was built to float on the water and this is its sole redeeming feature. For locals and tourists alike the three lanes can be a traffic bottleneck, and a new five-lane bridge is being constructed a few metres north of the present structure.

The second thing eastbound motorists and cyclists are likely to notice is a large area of trees, lawns, beaches and flowers immediately to the left (north) on the Kelowna side of the bridge. This is City Park, the heart of urban Okanagan.

City Park

The best way to get to know Kelowna and see its features is to start at City Park and take a stroll along the lakeshore. It can be done in an hour, but allow half a day if you are the curious sort.

The entrance to City Park off Abbott Street meanders through impressive rows of roses and other

and the board of the Armstrong agricultural fair, and being a Scotsman at heart, was active in curling clubs around the province. Before he died in 1939, Dun-Waters "sold" Fintry for one dollar to Fairbridge Farm Schools, an English charitable organization that sent orphans to the colonies where they could learn to be farmers and earn a living for themselves. The students continued to run the farm at Fintry for a number of years.

After passing through the hands of different owners and some years of disuse, Fintry was purchased by the provincial government in 1995 and a provincial park and protected area were created in the surrounding lands. The Friends of Fintry Provincial Park Society is slowly and meticulously restoring the house and grounds, which are open to tours, to their former glory. ◆

>>> The boardwalk near the Grand Hotel is popular with strollers and rollers.

flowers, a botanical bevy known officially as Veendam Gardens (Veendam, Netherlands, is one of Kelowna's sister cities). Ahead are public tennis courts, a lawn bowling green, war memorial, skateboard park, children's water park and a 1955 totem pole.

The sandy stretch at water's edge is called Hot Sands Beach, a name that is self-explanatory to barefoot bathers on summer afternoons. This is the best downtown swimming and sun-bathing spot.

Follow the sidewalk that runs parallel to the lake going north from City Park and you will go out of one park and into another. This pathway leads to *The Sails*, a sculpture that was

>>> The best downtown meeting place is at the Sails.

lowered into place by helicopter in 1977. With white wings stretching skyward like a schooner reaching for wind, *The Sails* is a favourite downtown meeting place and a perfect spot to people-watch.

A few dozen metres from the white sculpture is the Ogopogo statue that kids love to climb on.

The small space with grass and trees in front of the Ogopogo statue is Kerry Park, where musicians perform on many evenings in summer. The names and locations of quite a few of Kelowna's waterfront spots, such as Hot Sands Beach and Tugboat Bay, are spread by word of mouth, so don't bother to look for signs.

The 50-metre (155-foot) mock sternwheeler *Fintry Queen* (250-979-0223) has been a fixture on the Kelowna waterfront since 1949, when it started life as *Lequime*, a car ferry that shuttled vehicles across the lake before the bridge was built. Ten years later it was decommissioned and rebuilt to resemble a paddlewheeler. In recent years it has had financial difficulties and sailings have been irregular.

The lakeshore path expands into a divided biway that separates

<<< Kids like getting their pictures taken with the Ogopogo statue.

pedestrians from human-powered wheeled transport and passes Stuart Park and the yacht club before reaching the big hotel.

Grand Okanagan Lakefront Resort and Conference Centre is the full name of The Grand, a classy hotel housing an array of shops and a statue of three dolphins cavorting in a fountain. These black dolphins, named *Harmony*, are the centrepiece of the hotel's lobby. Nearby white dolphins, named *Rhapsody*, cavort in an outdoor fountain. Both statues were created by local sculptor by R. Dow Reid.

Waterfront Park

The hilly green space behind The Grand is Waterfront Park, which features several kilometres of paths interlaced with gardens, water-falls, lagoons, an amphitheatre and a lakeside boardwalk. The walk-way crosses one of the world's smallest nautical locks, roughly 10 metres (33 feet) long and 3.5 metres (10 feet) wide. Boaters who wish to travel between the lake and the lagoon phone for the locksmith, who opens the gates to flood the short canal and raise or lower their vessel a metre (3 feet) or so to make it the same level as the lagoon.

Continue along the boardwalk next to the lakeshore and you will come to a sandy beach known as Tugboat Bay and a bronze sculpture appropriately called *On the Beach*, by Kelowna sculptor Geert Maas. Here, tourists and residents alike will find any number of activities to amuse and entertain. All kinds of watercraft are available for rent, from sailboats to motorboats to Ogopogo paddleboats. Water skiing, parasail-ing, bike rentals and lake tours are just some of the available activities.

To exit the lakeshore, pass between two low buildings and follow the path over Harmony Bridge to the white dolphins statue, where you can start off to explore the downtown cultural district. Otherwise, continue along the lakeshore behind the new Discovery Bay condos to reach a nature-viewing area.

Wildlife Marsh

The lakeshore pathway ends at Brandt's Creek Estuary Restoration Project, a haven for such birds as blue herons, osprey, ducks and the ubiquitous Canada goose. Boardwalks lead out to the Rotary Marsh Wildlife Sanctuary, which includes viewing areas and information signs.

The main pathway leaves the lake, crosses Sunset Drive, dips under an oriental-style entry and then follows Brandt's Creek to Recreation Avenue. A great blue heron wading in the creek may catch your eye, but look again—it's a sculpture. A right turn at the end of the path leads to Ellis Street, where a right turn will take you past the library and museums to Bernard Avenue. A right turn at Bernard leads back to *The Sails* sculpture and the lake.

Museums and Galleries

Kelowna's museums, theatres and galleries are clustered downtown within an area known as the cultural district. Try this quick orientation tour that begins at the north end of Water Street just before it curves around the big arena called Prospera Place. The 6,000-seat arena, built in 1999, has hosted the likes of Elton John, Rod Stewart and Jose Carreras.

Kelowna Art Gallery

- 1315 Water Street
- 250-762-2226

At the junction of Water Street and Cawston Avenue a big wooden apple on the sidewalk marks the art gallery. The 15,000-square-foot gallery has three exhibition spaces where programs and displays constantly change, as well as a classroom and studio where visitors can drop in and create art.

Rotary Centre for the Arts

- 421 Cawston Avenue

A few steps along Cawston Avenue from the art gallery you can view dancers, artists and musicians practising their skills in studios at the Rotary Centre. Pottery and artisans' studios and music rooms share the space with a theatre, cafe and offices. The Alternator Gallery for Contemporary Art (250-868-2298) provides a venue for unorthodox or controversial art not usually exhibited in municipal or commercial galleries. There is no admission charge to the Rotary Centre so wander at will.

Laurel Packinghouse

• 1304 Ellis Street at Cawston

A shipping house for the fruit industry from 1917 until the 1970s, the Laurel Packinghouse, Kelowna's first designated heritage building, has been restored as the venue for two museums. The B.C. Orchard Industry Museum (a.k.a. the "apple museum") tells the story of the Okanagan Valley's transformation from cattle range to orchard. The Wine Museum and VQA Wine Shop are a must for the oenophile; the wine shop has wine for sale from virtually every Okanagan winery.

From behind the Rotary Centre, take a pleasant, shady stroll through a pergola that connects the centre to the public library on Ellis Street. Collages of old apple-box labels and sculptures of fruit enhance the pergola.

Okanagan Military Museum

• 1424 Ellis Street
• 250-763-9292

The Memorial Arena is typical of many small-town, post-Second World War Canadian hockey arenas. Step inside and you find the Military Museum, with exhibits from the Canadian Armed Forces, including small arms, uniforms, insignias, badges and equipment. The collection includes items from the Boer War through to more recent military operations.

Kelowna Museum

• 470 Queensway at Ellis
• 250-763-2417

Rotating exhibits, such as one in honour of Kelowna's centennial, share space with the permanent gallery of Okanagan and First Nations' artifacts. The museum focuses on the development and transformation of the city: visit Kelowna's Chinatown or step inside John McDougall's 1860s trading post. The Ethnography Gallery offers visitors a chance to explore collections from Central and South America, Asia, Oceania and Africa. Admission by donation.

>>> Bennett Clock is another great meeting place.

Bennett Clock
• Queensway Avenue

Around the corner from the museum the Bennett Clock honours former B.C. premier W.A.C. (Wacky) Bennett, who lived much of his life in Kelowna. The carillon clock's 20 pillars and 7 steps symbolize the 20 years and 7 terms Bennett served as premier. Try to time your visit for the top of the hour so you can hear the chimes.

Kasugai Gardens
A hidden gem, the Japanese-style Kasugai Gardens was designed as a symbol of the friendship between sister cities Kelowna and Kasugai, Japan. Tucked behind city hall and the Bennett Clock and protected by a wall, this treasure can be hard to locate without guidance. The tranquil spot is a perfect place for a brown-bag lunch or a moment of quiet contemplation.

Additional Attractions
B.C. Fruit Packers Co-operative
• 816 Clement Avenue
• 250-763-8872

Water Street curves around Prospera Place arena and becomes Clement Avenue where, at the Fruit Packers Co-op, you can find dozens of varieties of crisp apples that are sold for much less than elsewhere. Ask for a sample if you are curious about the taste of a certain variety. Reduced-price "juicers" are available at the back of the store for making apple juice or baking.

<<< Plump koi swim at Kasugai Gardens.

>>> Fruit Packers Co-operative offers apples aplenty.

Big White Ski Resort

• off Highway 33
• 250-765-3101, 800-663-2772

With 14,000 beds and 16 lifts Big White, about 45 minutes southeast of Kelowna, is the busiest snow resort on Highway 97. In the summer it is among the least active as it closes down and offers no activities.

Elysium Garden Nursery

• 2834 Belgo Road
• 250-491-1386

The Okanagan's only commercial display garden

Mail-Order Wheel

To get an idea of how the transportation system worked before the building of Highway 97 and other roads, let's take a look at the route taken by a stone grinding wheel that was ordered in 1871 by Frederick Brent of Kelowna for the Okanagan's first gristmill. He ordered it, probably by mail, from San Francisco where it was put on an ocean steamer to Victoria. A riverboat then took it up the Fraser River to Yale, where it was loaded onto a wagon and taken along the Cariboo Wagon Road to Cache Creek. At that point it departed the well-travelled route and branched off for Savona, on Kamloops Lake. From Savona it went back onto a ship that took it to the end of the lake and up the South Thompson River to Shuswap Lake and then up the Shuswap River to Enderby, about 95 kilometres (59 miles) north of its final destination.

Frederick Brent met his millstone at Enderby, loaded it onto a borrowed wagon and followed a narrow trail through the bush to the shore of Okanagan Lake near O'Keefe Ranch. In a small boat he then rowed the stone down the lake to Kelowna. But that wasn't the end of its trip. At Kelowna it was dragged onto a skid and pulled by horses to Brent's Grist Mill, which still stands and is the oldest industrial building in Kelowna and the oldest gristmill in the province. The mill building, along with the Brent farmhouse and dairy barn, has been relocated to a future heritage site at Dilworth Drive and Leckie Place in Kelowna. The wheel is in the Kelowna Museum. ◆

features thousands of perennials in an old apple orchard near rushing Mission Creek. The owners started planting in 1998 with the idea of showing the range of flowers that can be grown in the Okanagan. The beautiful and bountiful 1.3 hectares (3 acres) include a Japanese garden, xeriscape garden, nursery, plant sales and self-guided tours.

Father Pandosy Mission
- 3685 Benvoulin Road
- 250-860-8369

The mission was established in 1859 by Fathers Charles Pandosy and Pierre Richard, who were Oblate Catholic missionaries. The four original buildings are the brother's house, the chapel, the root house and the barn. The Christian house (named after the Christian family) and a log cabin have been moved to the site. A historic treasure, the mission is the earliest European settlement in the valley.

>>> Father Pandosy Mission is the Okanagan's first White settlement.

Floating Bridge
The attraction of the only bridge across Okanagan Lake is that it floats—the only one of its kind in Canada and one of very few in the world. It was built that way because of the extreme depth of the water and the soft lake bottom. The bridge's total span is just short of 1.6 kilometres (1 mile), while the floating section measures 640 metres

<<< Wilderness is found within Kelowna along Mission Creek.

(2,100 feet) and is constructed of pontoons that are 60 metres (200 feet) long and are submerged about 2.2 metres (8 feet). Ten regular pontoons plus two small end pontoons make up the floating section. Anchors weighing 70 tons are embedded into the lake bottom to hold everything in place.

Geert Maas Sculpture Gardens and Gallery

- 250 Reynolds Road
- 250-860-7012

Geert Maas's many works are on display at his semi-rural studio. Visitors can stroll among bronze, stone, steel and aluminium artwork outside and enjoy oils, acrylics, lacquers and smaller sculptures inside.

Guisachan Heritage Park

- 1060 Cameron Avenue

Built for the Earl and Countess of Aberdeen in 1891 and named for their family estate in Scotland, Guisachan is a Gaelic word meaning "place of the firs." The planted firs didn't survive the Okanagan climate, so they've been replaced with cedars. Guisachan House eventually became the focal point of a 200-hectare (480-acre) ranch. Extensive gardens that are open to the public free of charge surround the house and display an astounding variety of roses, herbs, annual and perennial flowers, shrubs and trees. The house and grounds are managed by the Central Okanagan Heritage Society, which also sponsors the Guisachan Garden Show the first weekend in July.

Kelowna Land and Orchard Company

- 3002 Dunster Road
- 250-763-1091

This 60-hectare (150-acre) working farm 15 minutes from downtown Kelowna was established in 1904. The apple orchard produces 2.5 million kilograms (6 million pounds) of fruit annually. Some of the farm's features are a petting zoo, wagon tours, the Farm Store, Raven Ridge Cidery and the Ridge Restaurant.

Knox Mountain

The base of Knox Mountain begins at the north end of Ellis Street. You will find the mountain access road beside the Tolko Industries wood processing plant, near a boat launch by Sutherland Park. The road winds towards the mountaintop, as do many pathways. Two viewing areas feature ramadas, viewpoints, signs and picnic areas. Other features include a children's play area, a secluded lake and countless hiking and biking paths. Views of the bridge, Westbank, the city and the lake north to Vernon are nothing less than spectacular. This is Kelowna's favourite recreation area with several trails leading from the uppermost parking area to two different summits. There are too many trails to describe, but since the mountain is within the city it is extremely difficult to get lost.

Okanagan Lavender Herb Farm

- 4380 Takla Road
- 250-764-7795

Enjoy self-guided tours, a self-pick and gift shop, all amid the glorious scent of the purple plants. Sixty varieties of lavender are grown in an area of rolling vineyards, orchards and oversized homes, so sightseeing in the area is interesting.

Rabbits on Enterprise Avenue

A few years ago some domestic rabbits gained freedom in northeast Kelowna and they have since bred, as rabbits will. The offspring come in every colour, size and shape that you would expect. The best time for viewings is at dawn and dusk, when the bunnies are most plentiful. They can be found on the lawns of businesses along Enterprise Way about a kilometre from Spall Road. This oddball attraction doesn't get into the tourist brochures but the kids will love seeing Bugs and friends.

Summerhill Pyramid Winery

- 4870 Chute Lake Road
- 250-764-8000

If you are only going to visit one vineyard on Highway 97, choose either this one or Mission Hill in Westbank. Summerhill has something for everyone, including a pyramid. Apparently the application of sacred geometry improves the flavour of wine, so the owners here have built a scientifically designed, properly oriented, 8 percent replica of the Great Pyramid at Cheops in which to store some vintages. They say the results have been proven by taste tests.

>>> Wine floats at Summerhill.

>>> Designer apples are sold at the Apple Fair.

Summerhill bills itself as "Canada's most visited winery and largest certified organic vineyard." While the adults amuse themselves with tasting, the kids can play in a parkette or bang the brass gong on the porch until their parents make them stop. The view over the lake is spectacular, but that in itself is not unusual for an Okanagan winery. Short strolls take visitors through grape vines to the pyramid, a Native earth house and a restored log cabin.

Events
Apple Fair

- Orchard Museum
- Laurel Building, 1304 Ellis Street
- Saturday in late October

As many as 20 varieties of apples are

available for sampling. Recipes and juice are handed out, while pies, candy apples and fresh-picked apples are for sale.

Farmers' and Crafters' Market
• Springfield Road and Dilworth Drive

On Saturday mornings 165 vendors and 5,000 customers converge, starting at 8 a.m. Look for painted rocks and homemade bread. The market also runs on summer Wednesday mornings, but with fewer vendors.

>>> Hand-painted rocks are among the crafts at Kelowna's Farmers' Market.

Field of Dreams car show
• City Park
• Friday and Saturday in mid-September

Auction, swap meet and car show with more than 1,000 exotic and antique cars. Included is a cruise-in at the Capri Mall on Friday and a sock hop at the Elk's Hall on Saturday.

Kelowna Dragon Boat Festival
• Waterfront Park
• three days in mid-September
• 250-868-1136, 888-309-5674

The big boats with 20 paddlers, a drummer and a helmsperson race in the second-biggest dragon-boat festival in B.C. Involved are 150 teams, 3,500 participants and too many spectators to count. No charge to watch or visit numerous booths and concessions at this lively event.

Family Fun Day
- Parkinson Recreation Centre, Harvey Avenue and Spall Road
- Sunday of May long weekend
- 250-860-3938

There is enough going on at Family Fun Day to keep preteen children amused for the afternoon—games, draws, prizes, competitions, awards, entertainment, activity tents and play areas indoors and out. For 20 years this has been one of the great family events of the Okanagan. And it's free.

Kelowna International Regatta
- many downtown locations
- mid-July

This weekend festival incorporates the Classic and Antique Boat Show as well as the Mardi Gras Street Festival. Bernard Avenue closes to vehicles and opens to a Saturday morning arcade, sidewalk sale, vendor booths, family fun activities and entertainment. Other features include boat building, wakeboarding, water skiing, a swim race, carnival rides, a cherry fair and dogs catching Frisbees. The event covers six city blocks and has three stages with entertainment.

Mayor's Environmental Expo
- Kerry Park
- end of May

Held in conjunction with National Environment Week, the Expo features demonstrations of cycling, efficient fireplaces, forest resources and other friendly and efficient energy savers. Kids events include the slow bike race and blending juice drinks with pedal power.

Snowfest
- City Park and other locations
- last week in January

Sno-pitch, water skiing, wakeboarding, outdoor volleyball, fireworks, a parade, dance and concerts plus a polar-bear dip in Okanagan Lake at Hot Sands Beach are all on the schedule. The event has been held for over 30 years, often without any snow. In a quest for the white stuff, the fest has recently been moved a week later to the end of January, when the weather is a bit more cooperative.

Wine Festivals
- Okanagan Wine Festivals Society
- 1527 Ellis Street
- 250-861-6654
- www.owfs.com

Four seasonal wine festivals are held throughout the Okanagan, and they are huge events that bring in bus- and plane-loads of generally affluent participants. While the festival is good for the wine businesses, the events are almost invisible to the public, as they occur at wineries, in restaurants and in seminar rooms. Events are normally priced from $35 to several hundred dollars. Occasionally a lecture or demonstration is offered for free.

Spring Wine Festival
- four days, including first weekend in May

More than 100 wine-related events, mostly dinners, tastings and seminars, are staged throughout the Okanagan, with the majority taking place south of Kelowna.

Fall Wine Festival
- 10 days in late September and early October

By far the biggest of the four festivals, the fall fest takes place during the heart of the grape harvest. The 165 events scattered throughout the valley focus on wine, food and education on how to combine the two. (See Vernon for the Summer Wine Festival at Silver Star, and Kamloops for the Ice Wine Festival at Sun Peaks.)

Tourist Info
Kelowna Chamber of Commerce
- 544 Harvey Avenue
- 250-861-1515
- www.tourismkelowna.com

97 LAKE COUNTRY >>> *population: 9,750*

An amalgamation of the communities of Oyama, Winfield, Okanagan Centre and Carr's Landing, Lake Country spreads along Highway 97 like an extension of Kelowna. Lake Country branches out into the benches above Okanagan Lake and Wood Lake, where many of the homes have spectacular views of the lakes and surrounding orchards.

Both Carr's Landing and Okanagan Centre were orchard settlements and former steamship landings on the east side of Okanagan Lake. Carr's Landing was settled by Andy Carr, who planted the area's first apple, pear and peach trees.

The townsite of Okanagan Centre, population 360, shoulders Okanagan Lake and is 20 kilometres (12 miles) north of Kelowna. It was a busy spot in 1908 with a hotel, store, post office and school. Grape and wine production have become important in this area.

Oyama's tiny commercial area straddles the causeway that separates Kalamalka Lake from Wood Lake. A canal connecting the two lakes runs under the road just east of Highway 97. Wood Lake was once a metre (3 feet) higher than Kalamalka Lake, but the man-made canal evened them out. Oyama, with 1,500 residents, got its name from Japanese Prince Iwao Oyama, a hero in the Russo-Japanese war (1904–5).

Oyama has two interesting attractions. A ramshackle building known as Okanagan Display and Store Fixtures sells commercial shelving, racks and lighting, but stuffed in nooks and crannies are antiques, collectibles and decor items that make rummaging fun. Kaloya Regional Park is a picturesque peninsula that juts into Kalamalka Lake. A trail around the perimeter of the park offers several swimming options. No sign directs visitors to this developed park, so from 97 go east across the causeway and turn north to the end of Trask Road.

Winfield is the biggest and southernmost of the Lake Country settlements, just beyond Kelowna and about 30 kilometres (18 miles) before Vernon. Winfield Lodge was the home of Thomas Wood, justice of the peace, stock raiser, homesteader and the source of Wood Lake's name. The village developed as a fruit-packing centre in the 1920s.

The title "Apple Capital of Canada" has been attributed to Lake Country, as has the claim that 35 percent of Canada's apples are grown here. This is another of the strange apple claims that pop up along Highway 97's corridor of orchards. The entire province of British Columbia produces about 35 percent of Canada's apples, although most do come from the Okanagan.

Attractions

Gibson Heritage House at Kopje Regional Park

• 15480 Carr's Landing Road

This lakefront acreage was purchased by George Gibson in 1906. The house he built in 1912 is now a restored museum furnished in the style of the times. In the park you can enjoy a self-guided tour, swimming beach, picnic area, playground and baseball diamond. The Gibson House Strawberry Tea is held in June.

Events

Artwalk

• Lake Country Community Complex in Winfield

• second weekend in September

Lake Country's indoor and outdoor display of quilts, paintings, sculptures, and other works of art runs all day for two days and is the biggest art show in the Interior of B.C.

>>> Artisans and buyers mingle at Lake Country's Artwalk.

Oyama Fun Day

- first weekend of June

Family fun includes a pancake breakfast, parade, silent auction, children's field events and a dunk tank.

Tourist Info

Lake Country Business Association

- 1-11852 Highway 97, Winfield
- 250-766-3876

 VERNON >>> *population: 36,500*

One of the first things a Vernon visitor notices is that the city has been painted—and not in plain pastels or institutional greens, but with colourful, dynamic murals.

Everywhere you go in downtown Vernon you come face to face with larger-than-life characters in huge paintings depicting the story of the community and its founders. Having taken the mural tour in Toppenish, Washington, Highway 97's other painted city, I can't say that one is better than the other. I can, however, say that it's a terrific way to brighten up a community and turn dull, ugly walls into vibrant works of art.

Vernon shares with Bend, Kamloops and Kelowna the honour of having the best downtown parks along 97. Polson Park offers a

<<< War support is a mural theme in this Vernon alley.

combination of culture, leisure, and athletics. It is on the right side as you descend the hill and enter downtown from the south so there is no problem finding it.

Vernon's setting is close to three lakes, but the main part of the city isn't quite on any of them. Swan Lake, to the north, is a shallow bird sanctuary. To the west, an arm of Okanagan Lake features Kin Beach and Paddlewheel Park. Kalamalka Lake, directly south, has summer amenities at Kal Beach. Both offer prime boating and bathing.

The growth of luxuriant bunchgrass attracted cattle ranchers to the Vernon area in the 1860s and 1870s. This now rare vegetation can still be sampled (looked at, not eaten) at Kalamalka Provincial Park.

O'Keefe Ranch, founded in 1867 by Cornelius O'Keefe, provides an example of an early ranch settlement. The early White settlers in this valley built huge ranches, and the ranch headquarters were self-contained communities.

Attractions
Allan Brooks Nature Centre
- 250 Allan Brooks Way
- 250-260-4227

The centre is a former Environment Canada weather station that sits atop a ridge overlooking the town. The view from the Brooks Centre is one of the few easily accessible points where Swan, Okanagan and Kalamalka lakes are all in plain view. Both inside and out, the centre is devoted to the exploration of the diverse natural world of the North Okanagan. The Habitat and Discovery rooms are geared towards children and school groups, but the hands-on activities are fascinating for big kids too. Stroll out onto the Grasslands Trail for a visit to Marmot City, or explore the native plants and habitat stewardship displays in the Naturescape Gardens. A scheduled interpretive program is also available for visitors. Allan Brooks, who came to the Okanagan in 1905, was a leading North American illustrator of avian life.

Davison Orchards
- 3111 Davison Road
- 250-549-3266

Set on 20 hectares (50 acres) overlooking Vernon, this family farm has been selling homegrown fruit, vegetables, flowers, apple pies and fresh apple juice since 1933. It features heritage displays, farm animals, a picnic area, children's play area and orchard tours.

Kalamalka Lake Provincial Park

- 8 kilometres (5 miles) south of Vernon, on the northeast side of Kalamalka Lake, off Kalamalka Road and Highway 6

Once noted as one of the 10 most beautiful lakes in the world by *National Geographic*, Kalamalka is what is known as a "marl lake," with limestone crystals in the water reflecting the sunlight and changes in water temperature creating ribbons of deep blue and emerald green.

The 978-hectare (2,400-acre) park is made up of rolling slopes and forested ridges of pine, fir and cottonwood, with plenty of natural wetlands and ponds. The variety of habitat makes this a prime birding location. Coyote, deer, Pacific rattlesnakes and black bear all live here, but you are more likely to see the rather forward Columbian ground squirrels and yellow-bellied marmots. The park has more than 10 kilometres (6 miles) of trails for biking, hiking and horseback riding. Scenic cliff-top viewpoints overlook a rocky shoreline indented with bays and tiny coves. The lake's name is a Salish word that translates to "lake of many colours."

Magnetic Hill

- 5300 Dixon Dam Road

Getting to the reversing hill between Hughes and Hartnell roads is tricky because there are no signs and if you approach from the wrong direction the effect is lessened. In downtown Vernon, turn east onto 43rd Avenue then left on Pleasant Valley Road. Two blocks later turn right on BX Road (also called 46th Avenue), which twists and turns and changes names constantly, next becoming East Vernon Road. At the sign for Briggs Road go left. After a sharp turn, the road becomes Dixon Dam Road. Continue for less than a kilometre (.6 miles) and turn left at the sign for Dixon Dam Road (it continues straight ahead as Hartnell). Shortly you will overlook a valley. Stop your vehicle about 100 metres on, just as you start to go down a slight hill. Put the car in neutral, and, amazingly, you will apparently start to coast backwards up the hill that you thought you were going down. Magnetic Hill B&B is just ahead, on the left—if you reach it you have gone too far.

Okanagan Science Centre

- 2704 Highway 6
- 250-545-3644

Two complementary components here—fun and education—are aimed at kids, with two major exhibits, such as chemistry and electricity, changing every few months so there is always something new. The Discovery Room is a hands-on lab where young guests can conduct experiments and projects in such areas as structures, machines and physics. The centre is adjacent to Polson Park, so it is easily included in a family outing.

O'Keefe Ranch

- 12 kilometres (8 miles) north of Vernon on Highway 97
- 250-542-7868

Founded in 1867 by Cornelius O'Keefe, this prosperous cattle ranch once spread over 8,000 hectares (20,000 acres) of prime Okanagan land. Cornelius made his first money as a drover, herding cattle purchased for $15 a head in Oregon across the Columbia and Fraser rivers and over mountain ranges to the gold-mining communities in the Cariboo, where they fetched $150 apiece.

The ranch features tours of the restored O'Keefe home and self-guided walks to a working blacksmith shop, schoolhouse, saddle-making shop, St. Anne's Church, general store, cookhouse, post office and museum. A continuous calendar of weekend activities includes horse shows, a motorcycle rally, a muscle car show, an antique farm equipment display and Cornelius O'Keefe Days and Cowboy Festival in late July.

O'Keefe Ranch has an original stagecoach from the BX line as well as a rubber-tired replica that it uses for rides and parades. The BX connected O'Keefe Ranch to Kamloops and the Cariboo.

Okanagan Opal Inc.

- 7879 Highway 97
- 250-542-1103

The showroom at the north end of Vernon displays many types of opals, including locally named Kalamalka crystal and Okanagan wildfire. To find your own opals, you can join a weekend convoy that goes to the mine 40 kilometres (25 miles) west of Vernon.

Paddlewheel Park

- between Okanagan Landing Road and Okanagan Lake

The 1886 terminus for the Shuswap–Okanagan Railway and the former CPR-line shipbuilding site is home to the Okanagan Landing Railway Station, Smith House and the 1892 Vernon Court House. Paddlewheel Park offers a sandy beach, grassed areas, a playground, basketball court, sand volleyball courts, tennis court, a boat launch and boat trailer parking. The annual Okanagan Landing Regatta takes place here in July.

Polson Park

- junction of Highways 97 and 6, in the south part of town

With trees, a brook and lots of green grass, the park is the perfect spot for a picnic, a stroll or a game. It has tennis courts, a lawn bowling green, a water park and play area for kids, sports fields, walking paths, Japanese gardens, a floral clock and a bandshell. The Okanagan Science Centre and the Vernon Art Gallery are adjacent and Vernon Creek trickles through it.

Silver Star Mountain Resort

- Silver Star Road
- 800-663-4431

Long after the skiers and boarders have made their last run, the mountain reopens for summer with wildflower and mushroom tours. A chairlift takes bikers and hikers to the summit for spectacular views and exciting descents. There is also a climbing wall, horseback riding and mountain-bike rentals. In winter it is the Okanagan's second biggest skiing and snowboarding area.

Spirit of the Okanagan

- 250-545-8388

Boat cruises of Okanagan Lake aboard the *Spirit of the Okanagan* start from Paddlewheel Park.

Vernon Art Gallery

- 3228 31st Street

More than 27,000 visitors each year view exhibits by local and guest artists in a gallery founded in 1945. It has a permanent collection of

500 works by local artists including Allan Brooks. On Tuesdays visitors can bring their lunch to Art Break from 12:10 to 1 p.m., and enjoy a short film or a talk related to the current exhibition.

Vernon Museum and Archives
- 3009 32nd Avenue
- 250-542-3142

Artifacts interpret the natural history, Native history and growth and development of the region. A good source for information on walking and driving tours of the historic and heritage sites in the Vernon area. The museum also has a large collection of Kettle Valley Railway memorabilia.

Events
Cornelius O'Keefe Days and Cowboy Festival
- O'Keefe Ranch
- 9380 Highway 97 N.
- last weekend of July
- 250-542-7868

The cowboy way of life is celebrated with poetry, music, a rodeo, cowboy theatre, western art show, dog demonstrations and a Wild West show.

Creative Chaos Craft Fair
- Recreation Complex
- first weekend in June
- 250-545-6963

The largest arts and crafts sale in western Canada has more than 200 artisans and crafters showing and selling their wares. Specialty foods, outdoor creative activities, local performing arts and Students' Showcase.

B.C. Open Gold Panning Championships and Family Fun Day
- Gold Panner Campground, Cherryville
- 37 kilometres (23 miles) east of Vernon
- May long weekend
- 250-503-1035

Cherryville hosts the panning championships where everyone from tots to professionals can try their hand at the gold-pan toss, pay-dirt toss, gold rush, claim stake and metal detecting and then relax with some barbecue and bannock baking.

Sunshine Festival

- downtown
- mid-June

Billed as one of the largest sidewalk sales in British Columbia, the festival fills the streets with up to 10,000 people who come to enjoy the music, buy the merchandise, watch the adventure demonstrations and eat lots of food.

Summer Wine Festival

- Silver Star Mountain Resort
- second weekend of August
- www.owfs.com

Set in a colourful, Victorian-style mountain resort with an abundance of alpine wildflowers, the festival features wine education, arts, music, tasting, evening entertainment, seminars, mile-high outdoor recreation and presentations by local artists.

Vernon Winter Carnival

- 10 days beginning first Friday in February
- 250-545-2236

The carnival includes the Hot Air Balloon Fiesta, ski races at Silver Star, ice and snow sculptures, a sno-pitch ball tournament, Frisbee golf, nighttime cross-country skiing by oil lamp, music and food. Take in the region's biggest parade on Saturday at noon, downtown.

Tourist Info (two locations)

- Watson House, 701 Highway 97 S.
- 250-542-1415, 800-665-0795
- 6326 Highway 97 N.
- 250-542-1415

 DETOUR >>> **NORTH ON 97A TO SHUSWAP**

A dozen kilometres north of Vernon, Highway 97 turns northwest to Kamloops while 97A continues north to some interesting towns that are worth a visit. Since many readers will be making the trip in both directions, 97A is a worthy alternate route and offers excellent scenery.

Highway 97B branches off from 97A and goes into Salmon Arm.

The Trans-Canada Highway links Salmon Arm and Kamloops, where you can rejoin 97. Let's give 97A and B some deserved attention and keep heading north from Vernon into Shuswap vacation country for a quick look around. The first town north of Vernon is Armstrong.

97A B.C. ARMSTRONG >>> *population: 4,200*

Just a couple of kilometres north of Armstrong is a significant spot known as the Okanagan Great Divide. South of it all surface water flows into the Columbia River and then into the Pacific Ocean. North of it the water flows to the Thompson and Fraser rivers and into the Pacific at Vancouver.

When work was completed on the Shuswap/Okanagan Railway in 1892, the settlement of Armstrong consisted of a lone boxcar that served as railway station and home for the rail agent. Lansdowne, a considerably larger settlement, had been bypassed by the rail line, so the citizens of that community picked up their buildings and quickly resettled beside the tracks in Armstrong, where the railway still bisects the centre of the old-fashioned western town. Trains still rumble through town occasionally, including a steam train from Kamloops.

>>> The Armstrong cheese tradition continues.

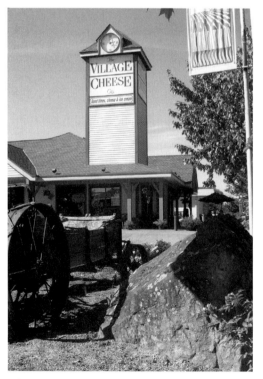

Armstrong has long been known for its cheese and at one point was the second-largest cheese producer in Canada. The Armstrong brand is now made in several Canadian factories and is, ironically, trucked to Armstrong.

Attractions
Village Cheese Company
• 3475 Smith Drive
• 888-633-8899

This modern facility carries on the tradition of Armstrong

cheese-making. It's located under the clock in the new part of town close to the highway. Here visitors can watch cheese being made in vats and sample chocolate cheese, blueberry cheese, goats' milk cheese, beer cheese and other interesting flavours.

Armstrong/Spallumcheen Museum and Art Gallery

- Pleasant Valley Road
- 250-546-8318

Area history is explained in the museum and the attached art gallery displays local artists' works. The museum has a reproduction of a train station, schoolroom, blacksmith shop and general store that brings back memories for some and educates others.

Chickadee Ridge Miniatures

- 1403 McLeod Road
- 250-546-9323

Miniature horses are the main attraction here, but there are also little donkeys, goats, sheep, cows and bunnies, plus various birds, from tiny quail and doves to huge emus, pheasants, peacocks and wild turkeys. Chickadee Ridge describes itself as "the largest miniature horse-breeding farm in Canada."

Caravan Farm Theatre

- 4886 Salmon River Road
- 10 kilometres (6 miles) N.W. of Armstrong
- 866-546-8533

A combination Clydesdale stud farm and live theatre venue, the Caravan has been entertaining audiences young and old since 1978. Productions are staged outdoors in all areas of the farm—a field, barn, forest or riding ring. The plays are designed for a family audience and run the gamut from adaptations of Shakespeare and Brecht to original musical and dramatic works. The winter sleigh-ride show always plays to sold-out crowds.

Farmers' Market

- Saturdays, 8 a.m. to noon

Held seasonally at the exhibition grounds in Armstrong.

Starlight Drive-In Theatre

- 933 Highway 97, between Enderby and Armstrong
- 250-838-6757

Before drive-in banking and fast foods, the term drive-in meant one thing—a place where you sat in your car and watched movies on a distant screen while sound crackled from a metal box hung from the car window. Families bundled up the kids, who soon fell asleep, and young couples went with the intention of not spending a lot of time watching the movie. Other than the sound coming through the car's FM radio, little has changed at the Starlight. It even shows double features, so an evening at the drive-in can last four or five hours. There are very few drive-in theatres left in North America, but two of them are on B.C.'s Highway 97. The other is in Prince George.

Events

Interior Provincial Exhibition and Stampede

- five days before the first weekend in September, but closed the holiday Monday
- 250-546-9406

Commonly known as the Armstrong Fair, this huge agricultural exhibition features heavy and light horses, a four-day rodeo, a parade and the largest midway in the province outside of Vancouver. Attendance is close to 90,000 and many events sell out. It has been operating for almost 110 years.

Tourist Info

Armstrong Chamber of Commerce

- 3550 Bridge Street
- 250-546-8155
- www.armstrongbc.com

 ENDERBY >>> *population: 2,800*

Originally called Lambly's Landing or Steamboat Landing, the name of this village just north of Armstrong came about in the late 1880s. Needing a name for their newly minted postmark, the citizenry debated their options. A local literary group became enthralled by a Jean Ingelow poem about rising waters: "The villagers were saved by the chiming of the church bells playing the tune 'The Brides of Enderby.'" When the post office opened that fall, many residents were surprised to learn that they were suddenly living in Enderby.

<<< Scenery and flowing water are Enderby attractions.

Attractions
Jim Watt Heritage Riverwalk
Enderby offers a pleasant walk along a paved path that follows the Shuswap River for 1.4 kilometres (nearly a mile). This is a favourite place for locals to cool off by floating on the river on rafts and tubes between the park and the bridge. Signage describes how the river was once a major transportation route.

Enderby and District Museum
- 901 George Street
- 250-838-7170

The 35-year-old museum's collection emphasizes local heritage with archives and a large assortment of photos, and interprets the human and natural history of Enderby and surrounding district.

Tourist Info
Enderby Chamber of Commerce
- 700 Railway Avenue
- 250-838-6727

 SALMON ARM >>> *population: 16,500*

The largest city in the Shuswap, Salmon Arm is home to the longest freshwater wharf in B.C. It reaches beyond the shallows of Shuswap Lake to provide houseboats and powerboats with a place to dock. Despite the abundance of surrounding water, Salmon Arm is not a

The Overlanders

In June of 1862 a group of 150 men and a pregnant woman, Catherine O'Hare Schubert, and her three young children, came across the country from Fort Garry (now Winnipeg) in ox-drawn Red River carts in search of Cariboo gold. These Overlanders endured incredible hardships, with injuries and death. When they were finally within reach of the goldfields, most were too exhausted to continue the trek to the Cariboo and in any event, they had discarded or traded away their heavy mining tools. Some of the survivors went down the Fraser River and headed for civilization at Victoria, some returned to the east and some stayed and turned to farming.

Catherine O'Hare Schubert gave birth to her fourth child on the shores of the Thompson River. Her husband, Augustus, was one of the few Overlanders who managed to eke out a living finding small quantities of gold. The Schuberts eventually began farming near Armstrong, where the town has erected a memorial in the park to an amazing and courageous woman who was determined to keep her family together.

natural harbour or recreational waterfront.

The town's name relates to its position at the head of the southern arm of Shuswap Lake on the flood plain of the Salmon River.

Attractions
Deep Creek Tool Museum

- 91 Deep Creek Road
- 250-832-2506

This rural repository of hand tools, modern and outdated, common and obscure, spreads around the outside of a rural residence and fills the garage and an adjoining room. On display are something like 4,000 wrenches, chainsaws, outboard motors, cherry pitters, toasters, scales and toys. The admission fee is extremely modest and proprietor Herb Higginbottom's enthusiasm is infectious as he gives personal tours that can last as long as the customer wants.

>>> Obscure and outdated devices can be tried at the Tool Museum.

Dock Walk

A short walk on the longest freshwater dock in British Columbia (I've seen it described as the longest in North America) is a must. Watching the houseboats come and go is always interesting, and

<<< Salmon Arm's long dock offers families a short walk.

on many summer evenings there are musical performances at a small bandstand.

Waterfront trails in both directions follow the lakeshore from the dock and lead to excellent birdwatching areas, including one with a viewing shelter. Much of the wetland is being exploited by developers, who are replacing the natural walkway with an elevated concrete sidewalk. The trail that goes eastward is about 4 kilometres (2.5 miles) long and used by hikers and bikers.

R.J. Haney Heritage Park

- junction of Highway 97B and the Trans-Canada Highway
- 250-832-5243

Nostalgia, history and heritage are at the forefront of this prime attraction. There is no admission charge to visit the restored buildings, which represent an era just after the turn of the 20th century. Set on 15 rolling hectares (40 acres), the buildings include a school, tea room, gas station, blacksmith shop, candy store, museum, log cabin, fire hall and home. Dinner theatre is held here twice a week in summer.

Events
Air Affair

- Salmon Arm Airport
- Father's Day (late June)
- 250-675-4895

Hosted by the Shuswap Flying Club, the Air Affair displays helicopters, ultralights, paragliders and other planes, plus a flea market, trade show and pancake breakfast.

Farmers' Market

- Piccadilly Mall parking lot
- Tuesday and Friday, 8 a.m. to 12:30 p.m.

Fresh produce from local farms is sold.

Grebe Festival

- Rotary Peace Park and public dock
- late May
- 800-661-4800

The nesting of the western grebe is the focus here. This small, crane-like marshland dweller nests in only two locations in B.C., one of which is Salmon Arm. The grebes arrive in April to make their nests among the reeds and grasses in the marshy water of the Salmon Arm bay of Shuswap Lake. During mating, two adults pair up and skim across the water in a romantic dance. B.C. Wildlife Watch provides a viewing area.

Salmon Arm Fall Fair

- Fairgrounds next to Blackburn Park
- mid-September

For close to 110 years, the fair has featured local arts and crafts, farm-animal competitions, commercial exhibits and a Saturday morning parade through town.

Salmon Arm Roots and Blues Festival

- mid-August weekend
- Salmon Arm Fairgrounds
- 250-833-4096

Six stages provide festival goers with an eclectic mix of music from around the world. Performances run Friday through Sunday and include many daytime and kid-friendly events, plus the headliner evening stage. On-site camping is available.

Salmon Arm Rodeo

- Fairgrounds
- mid-July weekend
- 250-833-4031

This classic, small-town rodeo features all the traditional events such as bull riding, saddle bronc, bareback and barrel racing.

Tourist Info
Salmon Arm Chamber of Commerce

- 200 Trans-Canada Highway S.W.
- 250-832-2230, 877-725-6667

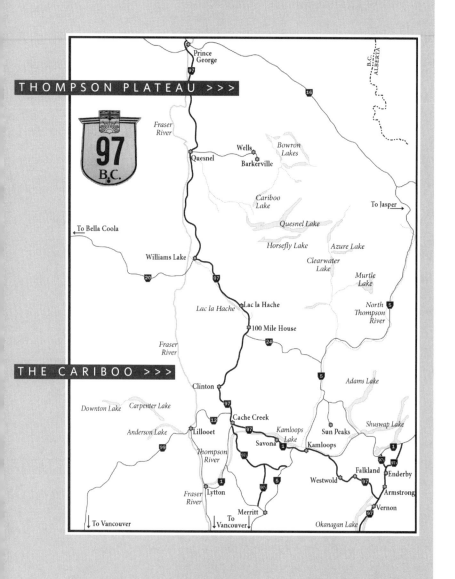

THOMPSON PLATEAU >>>

THE CARIBOO >>>

CHAPTER FOUR

Thompson Plateau and the Cariboo

On the Road to Falkland

IN CONTRAST TO THE HIGH DESERT IN THE UNITED STATES, THE COLUMBIA River gorge and the mountains of the Okanagan, you are now entering a region of low relief. Large portions of the Thompson Plateau undulate only a few hundred feet in altitude over very wide areas. This unusual (for B.C.) terrain presents spectacular scenery in two forms. First, from a few vantage points, the gently rolling land seems to stretch endlessly. Second, many of the region's rivers have cut into the plateau, leaving deep, rugged canyons.

Back on 97 after leaving Vernon, you also leave behind the lakes of the Okanagan, but discover new waterways that are beautiful if not as spectacular. As you approach the town of Falkland, 42 kilometres (26 miles) northwest of Vernon, keep your eyes left and notice what appears to be a gas station left over from about 1940. This display is a private collection; however feel free to stop, admire and photograph it.

FALKLAND >>> *population: 650*

Two things make this tiny hamlet stand out among the thousands of similar villages that go unnoticed in North America. Most people in the Interior of British Columbia know about the Falkland Stampede, the annual rodeo that has been going strong for nearly 90 years and is

>>> An old
service station,
seen from 97.

held on the May long weekend. Falkland's other claim to fame is the
biggest flag in western Canada. More of a billboard than a flag, it is
attached to a hillside above the town. At 9 by 12 metres (28 by 50 feet),
the painted flag is a tad smaller than the giant Stars and Stripes that
floats above Dorris, Oregon. Nevertheless it's Canadian, and it's big.
The proud people of Falkland are flag wavers and consider themselves
collectively "the most patriotic community in Canada." About 40
maple-leaf flags adorn the tiny downtown, and almost every public
celebration is cause to wave the red and white.

Attractions
Heritage Park Museum and Archives
• on Highway 97
• 250-379-2535

The .8 hectare (2-acre) park has log cabins, a caboose, barn, church
and traditional pioneer businesses. The collection is eclectic and interesting, with gypsum boulders strewn here and there as reminders of
the town's days as a mining centre. The museum has several wood-
burning heaters of unusual design. Admission by donation.

On the Road to Kamloops

The countryside is quiet and rolling, and Monte Lake, 50 kilometres
(31 miles) outside of Kamloops, is a perfectly pleasant place to stop for

<<< Heritage Park has ties to early automobiles.

a picnic and swim. At the far northwest end there is a nice stopping spot, but just beyond that point a road continues along the far end of the lake and provides seclusion and quiet. One sunny day I stopped here and some friendly campers pointed out a kingfisher, osprey and golden eagle, all perched in the trees next to the lake.

After winding around more hills, 97 flattens out in the farming community of Westwold and then has a brief relationship with the Trans-Canada Highway as they both follow the south shore of the South Thompson River, rushing towards Kamloops. At Lafarge Road

<<< A storm races across the South Thompson River.

on the right, a bridge allows for a crossing of this big river and a continuation into Kamloops on the north shore. This route is a much more enjoyable drive because there is hardly any traffic on the narrow stretch of blacktop.

 KAMLOOPS >>> *population: 80,000*

The odd name for the second biggest community on Highway 97 is a Native word meaning "meeting of the waters." The Thompson River forms here at the confluence of the North and South Thompson rivers. There are two other convergences, both vehicular in nature. The city is at the junction of the Trans-Canada, Yellowhead, Coquihalla and 97 highways. Additionally, it is the first place west of Winnipeg where both national railways meet.

Kamloops is one of several B.C. cities that boast a first-class park right in the heart of town. A short stroll from downtown across the railway tracks, Riverside Park's amenities read like a checklist for the perfect city oasis. Rose gardens, sculptures, a riverside walk, tennis courts, lawn bowling, a children's water park, swimming area, bandshell, Japanese gardens and numerous hiking and biking paths make it a delightful place to spend a day. Every summer evening, free concerts are held at the bandshell and can attract up to 1,000 listeners, who relax on blankets and lawn chairs.

>>> "Riverside City" promotes its perfect park.

The city bills itself as both the "Riverside City" and the "Tournament Capital of Canada." The former is clear, while the latter refers to an expanding list of facilities for competitive sports like baseball, golf, hockey and others. Kamloops could also be called the "Nickname City," since the titles "B.C.'s Original Hub City" and "Canada's Oldest Cowtown" have also been applied to it from time to time.

Surrounded by grassland and typical cowboy-country scenery, Kamloops is the economic centre of B.C.'s cattle industry.

Attractions
B.C. Wildlife Park
- 9077 East Dallas Drive
- 250-573-3242

The transition from zoo to home for native fauna is nearly complete at the Wildlife Park, although a few out-of-context creatures, such as a Siberian tiger, remain. The revitalized 40-hectare (120-acre) park is home to 65 species of local and endangered wildlife, and frequently offers presentations about falcons, bats and other interesting creatures. There are interpretive programs for kids at the Cactus Corral Children's Area, and the Wildlife Express miniature train clickety-clacks through the park, which remains open 364 days per year.

Kamloops Art Gallery
- 465 Victoria Street
- 250-828-3543

Big, bright and airy, this modern building next to the library hosts displays by British Columbia artists. The gallery has a permanent collection of local artists, with more than 1,000 works. About 25 exhibitions that examine social and cultural issues are held each year.

Kamloops Heritage Railway
- 6-510 Lorne Street
- 250-374-2141

On summer evenings the Spirit of Kamloops, an immaculately restored 2141 steam locomotive, puffs out of the old downtown Canadian National station. The 1912 engine pulls two open cars and a heritage coach across the South Thompson River and then chugs north of the city on a 75-minute journey. Along the way the train is

likely to be robbed of its gold by legendary Bill Miner and his gang of thieves on horseback.

Next to the station a small train museum doubles as the ticket booth. Watch for a special that combines the train ride with a meal at The Keg restaurant in the restored station. A recent addition to the schedule is a full-day, 185-kilometre (115-mile) return trip to Armstrong featuring a 160-metre (493-foot) tunnel, a unique horse-shoe curve, three rural communities (Monte Creek, Falkland and Westwold) and three crossings of Highway 97.

Kamloops Museum

- 207 Seymour Street
- 250-828-3576

Local Native culture, the fur trade, pioneer days, natural history, industry and transportation are all covered. You'll see a furnished turn-of-the-century living area, a stable complete with tack and carriage, a blacksmith shop, paddlewheels and old wall clocks and cameras.

Mountain Biking

Pick up the *Kamloops Visitors Guide* and they are on the cover. Another pair is on the *Kamloops Adventure Guide*. And they appear again on the tourism brochure. What are they? Mountain bikers—charging down the arid terrain of this city, which has taken to the relatively new sport like dirt to an oily chain.

This city is so enamoured of the influx of tourists attracted by off-road biking that it is creating a mountain-biking park conveniently close to the city and useable by all levels of riders. Sun Peaks Resort also takes cyclists to the top of its mountains on chairlifts.

<<< At the start—or end—of Highway 97, the small town of Weed, California, nestles among snow-capped mountains and coniferous forests.

<<< The Klamath Falls area contains vital stopover, nesting and refuelling sites for migratory waterfowl travelling the Pacific Flyway, such as these buffleheads.

>>> Eight miles past Redmond at the Peter Skene Ogden viewpoint you can look down into the dramatically steep Crooked River canyon and walk across an old bridge that used to support Highway 97.

>>> The Maryhill Stonehenge, built as a war memorial by Sam Hill, is a full-scale replica of England's famous and mysterious Stonehenge.

<<< Sam Hill's castle-like Maryhill Museum, situated on a large estate overlooking the Columbia River Gorge, features art and road-building memorabilia.

<<< Colourful murals depict the history of the Toppenish community; some are so expertly painted that they seem to be part of the landscape.

>>> Ellensburg's historic shopping district featuring six blocks of late-Victorian brick buildings looks like it was lifted right out of the movies.

>>> Near Brewster, the Okanogan River merges with the mighty Columbia.

<<< If only one winery is on your Oliver itinerary, Tinhorn Creek Vineyards is a good choice.

<<< Learn about planting techniques, diseases and harvesting at the demonstration vineyard next to the Tinhorn Creek Vineyards' main building.

>>> Highway 97N near Summerland offers dramatic scenic vistas.

>>> Westbank's Gellatly Nut Farm, Canada's first commercial nut orchard, has 100-year-old trees and a long stretch of lakeshore, a playground and a few heritage buildings.

<<< A 10-minute walk along a twisting path leads to Hardy Falls, 4 kilometres south of Peachland. The 10-metre waterfall fills a gorge with cool mist, and you can wade on the rocky creekbed.

<<< Mission Hill Family Estate Winery is built in the style of a Moorish castle and features a 12-storey bell tower with four bronze bells handcrafted in France.

>>> Arrow-leaf balsam graces Dilworth Mountain with a riot of colour in the spring.

>>> The Kelowna Dragon Boat Festival, the second-largest one in B.C., features big boats, each with 20 paddlers, a drummer and a helmsperson.

<<< This bridge is part of the scenic Mission Creek Greenway, a gravel-surfaced multi-use trail that can be accessed from along Lakeshore Road in downtown Kelowna.

<<< Once noted as one of the 10 most beautiful lakes in the world by *National Geographic*, Kalamalka is a "marl lake." Limestone crystals in the water reflect the sunlight, and changes in water temperature create ribbons of deep blue and emerald green.

>>> Storm clouds gather dramatically over the South Thompson River near Kamloops.

>>> At Enderby, a 1.4-kilometre paved path follows the Shuswap River, a great place to cool off by floating on rafts and tubes.

<<< Beautiful Salmon Arm is the largest city in the Shuswap area.

<<< This colourful canyon is about 16 kilometres north of Clinton. Like a miniature Grand Canyon, the Painted Chasm's walls are made of striated layers of rock in varying hues of greens and browns.

>>> Highway 20 (the Chilcotin Highway) links mainland B.C. to the Pacific Ocean. It intersects Highway 97 at Williams Lake and provides access to Tweedsmuir Provincial Park and Bella Coola.

>>> North of Prince George, the pastoral vistas are delightful.

<<< Dawson Creek began to blossom when American soldiers building the Alaska Highway camped here in 1942. The town still evokes the feeling of being on the cusp of the frontier.

<<< Bright yellow fields of canola brighten the summer landscape near Fort St. John. About 90 percent of B.C.'s canola is grown in the Peace region.

>>> Said to be the only curved wooden bridge in Canada, the Kiskatinaw Bridge, halfway between Dawson Creek and Fort St. John, is the only remaining original bridge on the Alaska Highway.

>>> This vista of the Peace River and its steep valley is breathtaking.

<<< Named after British admiral Horatio Nelson, Fort Nelson was established over 200 years ago as a trading post, but it didn't grow much until the Alaska Highway (shown here) was pushed through.

>>> Up to 2 metres tall, 4 metres long and 800 kilograms in weight, the hairy wild bison claims the road as its own. The bison were saved from extinction and now number 100,000 in Canada.

>>> Caribou eke out an existence in some of the world's most difficult and unforgiving terrain. They are related to Europe's reindeer.

Ranch Vacations

Kamloops is ranch country and that means ranch vacations and ranch-style accommodation are part of the landscape. The South Thompson Inn and Conference Centre is typical, its white buildings visible from 97/1 across the river that gives it its name.

Secwepemc Museum and Heritage Park

- 202-355 Yellowhead Highway
- 250-828-9801

White settlers had trouble with this tricky name (sa-kwep-mc) which means "the people," so they settled for Shuswap, which is the name of the combined 17 Native tribes in the Southern Interior. The museum displays Native crafts and photographs of life at the turn of the century. The ethnobotanical garden is full of plants and trees that were important in Native culture and nutrition. Powwows are occasionally held in the outdoor arena.

Sunmore Ginseng Factory

- 925 McGill Place
- 250-374-3011

A short factory tour, scheduled several times a day, tells about ginseng production and provides samples of the various by-products made from the herbal root. The factory has recently opened a ginseng spa designed according to the principles of feng shui. In your travels thus far you are likely to have seen planted fields with a black mesh material draped over them. That is a ginseng field and the mesh shades the plants from the sun.

Sun Peaks

- 1280 Alpine Road
- 250-578-7222, 800-807-3257

Of all the snow resorts along Highway 97, Sun Peaks, about 45 minutes north of Kamloops, is the most active in the summer. Sans snow, Sun Peaks offers swimming, golfing, tennis, chairlifts for hikers and bikers and canoeing in July and August.

Events
Ice Wine Festival

- Sun Peaks Resort

- mid-January

Dining, seminars and sampling the expensive Okanagan ice wines are the highlights of this festival set in a mountain ski village in the depths of winter. Ice wine is a rich, liqueur-like wine made from frozen grapes that must be harvested in below-freezing temperatures.

Kamloops Cowboy Festival
- Calvary Community Church
- mid-March
- 888-763-2224

Presented by the B.C. Cowboy Heritage Society, Canada's premiere cowboy heritage event has been going strong for a decade. A trade show, entertainment, poetry readings, the Western Art and Gear Show and about 30 exhibitors are on hand.

River Family Festival
- Riverside Park
- Sunday, mid-July

A free festival with a riot of things for kids to enjoy, including ice-cream-eating contests, pony rides, bungee run and laser tag. You can also take in live music, logger sports and a basketball tourney.

On the Road to Cache Creek

The Kamloops area is dry, desert-like terrain surrounded by bare hills and clay-coloured cliffs. Around every corner you expect to see John Wayne and the posse cutting off the bank robbers at the pass. As you head northwest and rise out of the low land, green coniferous forests gradually replace the brown, arid grasslands. The picturesque route follows the Thompson River, which widens into Kamloops Lake.

 SAVONA >>> *population: 650*

On the shore of Kamloops Lake sits the tiny community of Savona, best known locally for two gas stations that sell gas for quite a bit less than others in the area.

Originally on the north side of the lake, Savona was the stopping point for stagecoaches coming from the west. Passengers continuing east did so by steamboat. In 1885 the railway came to the south shore of Kamloops Lake, and in the winter of that year many buildings were pulled across the lake, on the ice, to create a new, relocated Savona, next to the tracks.

A rest stop at the top of Savona Hill offers a panoramic view of Kamloops Lake, the summer playground for Kamloops residents. Balancing Rock can be seen to the west, a huge boulder sitting atop a hoodoo pillar that has been eroded by thousands of years of wind and rain. Hoodoos are common in this part of the country. They are the tall columns of hard rock that stand nearly alone on cliffs and bluffs such as those beside the Thompson River. The surrounding softer rock has been eroded away.

A man from Corsica with the last name of Savona ran a ferry service across the end of Kamloops Lake; thus the euphonic name.

 CACHE CREEK >>> *population: 1,200*

Cache Creek owes its modern existence to the meeting of two roads, the Trans-Canada Highway and Highway 97. Sadly, this means that its main attractions are motels, restaurants and gas stations. It is difficult to find a reason to linger, other than to eat, sleep or fuel up, although some interesting festivals take place here during the year.

Unlike most of the communities along this stretch of 97, Cache Creek did not originate during the gold rush. At the time when prospectors populated the district, Cache Creek was still ranchland

<<< Hoodoos are common beside the Thompson River.

with the occasional homestead. The village only grew as the Fraser canyon road was paved and automobiles became the main mode of transportation. Prior to the advent of the Coquihalla Highway, most traffic heading north and east had to pass through Cache Creek.

Cache Creek adopted a 1950s and 1960s theme in the early 1990s to reflect its history as a flourishing mid-century transportation hub, but I find it hard to identify. A drive-in burger joint might qualify, but the green-trimmed motel seems to recreate an era with which I am not familiar. According to the tourism literature, the nostalgia theme can be found at the Dairy Queen Restaurant, Hungry Herbies Drive-In Restaurant, the North End Petrocan Restaurant, Bob's Recreational Sales and the Cariboo Jade Shoppe. See for yourself if any of these businesses take you back in time. The village has created a logo reminiscent of the era (it looks like a mid-50s Chevy) and has installed a three-sided neon sign with the logo at the main intersection.

>>> This welcome sign and display emphasize the transportation theme.

Interestingly, by accepting garbage from Vancouver, Cache Creek has become financially solvent and brags that it is one of the few debt-free communities in B.C. The landfill creates employment and the money has contributed to street improvements.

The name "Cache Creek" has two possible sources. One is that during the fur-trade era, supplies were stored—or cached—in the valley. The other is that after a stagecoach robbery, two bandits who were being chased by police buried their loot along the creek bed. One robber was killed and the other died later from his wounds, so their cache was never recovered.

Attractions
Bonaparte Bend Winery
- 2520 Cariboo Highway
- 250-457-6667

Fruit wines are produced from 10 different varieties of fruit grown on local orchards. Bonaparte claims to be Canada's most northern winery and it probably is. You would think that would make it North America's most northerly winery, except that there is a commercial wine maker in Alaska. Located a half-kilometre north of town on 97, the Bonaparte winery dates back to 1862.

Hat Creek Ranch
- 11 kilometres (7 miles) north of Cache Creek
- 250-457-9722

As a roadhouse on the old Cariboo Wagon Road, Hat Creek Ranch was an overnight stop for prospectors heading north to the goldfields. Restored buildings and a ride on a horse-drawn stagecoach along the path of the old road show what life was like both at a way station and en route. Also on the site are horseback trail rides, a Shuswap Native village, a blacksmith shop, roadhouse, barn and several other ranch buildings. Hat Creek House was built in 1861. The buildings have been restored to a 1901 standard.

<<< Life on the old roads can be relived at Hat Creek Ranch.

Cariboo Wagon Road to Gold

Next to the Alaska Highway, the Cariboo Wagon Road is probably the most famous and best documented section of Highway 97 in British Columbia; it is also the portion that is directly linked to B.C.'s biggest gold rush.

Two major gold rushes in B.C. affected the development of Highway 97. The first was in 1858 on the Fraser River and the other, in 1862, was farther north, in the Cariboo district. ("Cariboo," by the way, is simply the pioneers' erroneous spelling for the elk-like caribou.) Word spread about the riches to be found along the Fraser River when the Hudson's Bay Company shipped 800 ounces of gold to the mint in San Francisco in February of 1858. The gold was of little use in its raw state, and San Francisco had the closest mint. The city was very gold-conscious, and word quickly got out that British Columbia had a huge discovery.

Prospectors who could not afford the short ocean voyage to Victoria trekked through the Interior passes between mountain ranges, following old trails and making new ones. The search for gold on the Fraser River was a disappointment for the majority of miners, as the quest for gold often was. The men who did not return in disgust continued to pan their way up the various rivers, finding enough gold here and there to fuel new rumours of serendipitous finds. By 1862 they had reached the Cariboo. There, on Williams Creek east of Quesnel, Billy Barker struck gold. And good quantities of it.

A year later the town of Barkerville had grown up around the claim. It is said that Barkerville was briefly the biggest North American city north of San Francisco and west of Chicago. A

Events
Graffiti Days

- various locations
- second weekend in June

Named after the movie *American Graffiti*, this event is a tie-in to the town's 1950s and 1960s theme. Automobiles built before 1970 race at the nearby Nl'Akapxm Eagle Motorplex in the Old Time Drags competition. On Saturday afternoon the vehicles parade from the Motorplex through Ashcroft to Cache Creek Park. In the evening beside the community hall, the cars spin their tires to see who can burn the most rubber and create the most smoke. Bring breathing apparatus and earplugs. A sock-hop dance follows.

Tumbleweed Quilt Retreat

- Pentecostal Church
- April

Six days of quilting lessons and sessions are for all skill levels, with lots of seminars and demonstrations.

On the Road to Clinton

North of Cache Creek, the Cariboo Highway and 97 merge and run together as far as Prince George, where they again go their separate ways. This route rambles through the heart of the Cariboo region, with branch roads that lead into some of British Columbia's thinly populated outbacks.

The section of highway between Cache Creek and Prince George is slated to become four lanes. The trade-off is that as the road becomes safer, it will lose some of its motoring charm.

 CLINTON >>> *population: 750*

Like many other communities between Cache Creek and Prince George, Clinton was founded in

<<< Collectors and antique hunters will enjoy Clinton.

the 1860s as a roadhouse on the Cariboo Trail to serve prospectors and others headed to and from the goldfields. The town's original names were The Junction, Cut Off Valley and 47 Mile (the junction was 47 miles from Lillooet). In 1863, the town became Clinton in honour of Lord Henry Pelham Clinton, the colonial secretary of the day.

Once gold fever subsided, the ranching industry developed and then forestry became the mainstay of the economy in the 1950s. At one time 20 bush mills and sawmills operated in the area. Consolidation has led to only one surviving mill. Gas stations, motels and some interesting shops now anchor the town. For those with a special interest, the junk, collectibles and antique shops are worth some rummaging. Clinton and area is sometimes known as "The Guest Ranch Capital of British Columbia," but most of those destinations are situated well outside of the town itself.

Attractions
Clinton Museum
• 1421 Cariboo Highway

Built in 1892, the building that houses the museum served as a school until 1925, and then a courthouse from 1925 to 1955. It is of special interest because Circuit Judge Matthew Begbie (the "Hanging Judge") held court here (his desk is on display). Be

city of that size demanded supplies and getting them there was a formidable task. From Victoria, the men and equipment mostly travelled by steamship up the Fraser River to Yale, as far as the river was navigable. The paddlewheelers did a brisk business, but many impoverished miners and suppliers chose to walk on primitive trails or paddle canoes. Continuing from Yale involved 16-kilometre (10-mile) portages and narrow cliff-edge trails, making it almost impossible for bulky supplies to reach the miners. Many a horse, mule and person fell to their death en route. A road was needed.

The few British nationals who lived in western Canada were mainly Hudson's Bay Company workers and farmers who were overwhelmed by the hordes of gold seekers pouring in. They requested assistance from the Colonial Office in London, and help came in the form of a detachment of Royal Engineers who arrived from England after a four-month sail. Their duties were to do public works, survey townsites and build roads. As a military force, they would also stand guard and create a British presence in the colony to "promote a high social standard of civilization."

Occasionally referred to as "the eighth wonder of the world," the Cariboo Wagon Road started at Yale on the Fraser River and eventually ran nearly 600 kilometres (365 miles) north, then east to Barkerville. The first 6 miles, begun in May 1862, were the most difficult and were built by 200 Royal Engineers who blasted the steep rock cliffs of the Fraser Canyon and cut a road into its side. Where the rock fell away, perilous wooden bridges took the wagons from one

continued on following page

outcrop to another. The Alexandra Suspension Bridge, the first bridge of its type in the west, supported wagons and their teams of horses. Frightened passengers who crossed on the swaying platform watched the turbulent Fraser cascading below, no doubt fearing that they would join it.

The road was described as "utterly impassable for any animal but a man, a goat, or a dog." Nevertheless, by 1865, mule trains, freight wagons and stagecoaches served west-central British Columbia. The wagon road twisted through the Fraser Canyon, then on to Lytton, Lillooet, Quesnel and east to Barkerville. Towns along Highway 97 with names like 100 Mile House and 150 Mile House were overnight resting spots with roadhouses that got their names from their distances from Lillooet. Some of the original wagon road today lies beneath Highway 97 and the Trans-Canada Highway.

Construction Camels
One innovation tried during construction of the wagon road was the use of camels, which could carry heavier loads than mules. In 1862 Frank Laumeister, a prominent Victoria merchant and packer, brought 21 of these beasts of burden to Yale from railroad construction camps in Arizona.

Unfortunately, the sharp rocks were unkind to the camels' feet and many went lame. Other problems included an unpleasant odour from the Bactrians (Mongolian double-humpers) that caused horses to run away. The camels had many nasty habits. They kicked everything within reach, bit their

sure to tour the barn out back, which has some interesting machinery and photos. Admission by donation.

Painted Chasm
This colourful canyon 1.5 kilometres (1 mile) in length and 120 metres (130 yards) deep is easily reached via a short alternate route that follows the path of the original Cariboo Wagon Road. Exactly 16 kilometres (10 miles) north of Clinton, look carefully for Painted Chasm Road and turn right. In 4 kilometres (2.5 miles) you will reach an overview with a fence, which is actually a provincial park. Like a miniature Grand Canyon, the walls of the chasm are composed of striated layers of rock in varying hues of greens and browns. Below, the restrained trickle of Chasm Creek seems worn out by the tens of thousands of years it took to etch this huge cut into the relatively soft landscape.

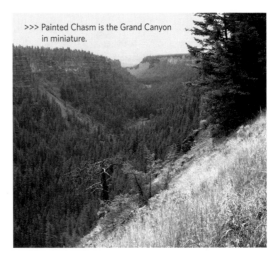

>>> Painted Chasm is the Grand Canyon in miniature.

To get back to 97, continue on for another 3 kilometres (less than 2 miles) and you will meet the highway, about 15 kilometres (9 miles) before a huddle of buildings known as 70 Mile House.

Palace Hotel

- 1418 Cariboo Highway

Downtown Clinton has preserved several historic buildings from the late 19th and early 20th centuries. The Palace Hotel was built in 1879 as the Le Forest residence, but Emile Le Forest sold the house and it became a hotel, catering to the freight drivers who stabled their animals in the large barn next door.

Robertson House

- 402 McDonald Avenue

Built in 1866, this house and its enlargement to a store was constructed from lumber obtained from the Smith family sawmill that was just behind the store, adjacent to Clinton Creek.

Sign park

- west side of Highway 97
- downtown Clinton

The tree stump with a truncated branch sticking out has been dubbed "the hanging tree." Posts are planted around it with attached signs that show the faded names of families and towns scribbled on them. I have asked about this display several times and the best explanation offered is "it's just something we did." So bring along your own shingle, nail it to a post and come back in a few years and it will likely be as faded as the others. Or save your shingle for the Sign Post Forest at Watson Lake, Yukon.

Events
Clinton Annual Ball
- Clinton Memorial Hall
- May long weekend

Clinton was only incorporated in 1963, but

keepers, ran away with their loads and enjoyed eating clothing, even while it was being worn. Eventually they died in accidents, were shot by hunters who mistook them for wildlife or were turned loose. Most of those that were turned loose eventually froze to death. These days a tame camel named Dundas with few bad habits can be found outside the Wells Hotel near Barkerville. His handler is happy to relate the history of camels in the Cariboo to curious visitors. ♦

<<< Clinton's sign park has no explanation.

The Hanging Judge

By the mid-1850s the California gold rush was over. The state had joined the Union, and the reasons that the quest for gold was such an adventure—no fences, no land ownership, no taxes, no authority—were the same reasons that crime became attractive. That, and the fact that impoverished and disillusioned young men, beyond the reach of family influence, were free to do as they pleased, anonymously, in the Wild West. Jails, previously unnecessary, were filled. Hangings became common, almost matter of fact.

John Bucroft, a cowboy gone bad, wrote home with the following casual message: "I take this opportunity of writing these few lines to you hoping to find you in good health. Me and Charley is sentenced to be hung at five o'clock for a robbery. Give my best to Frank and Sam."

This American lawlessness produced some of the frontier's most colourful characters, including the "Hanging Judge," Matthew Begbie. He was the first judge in mainland British Columbia and he saw his job as preventing the thievery and murder so prevalent south of the border from spreading north. A fearsome figure at 195 centimetres (6 feet 4 inches) tall, with a Van Dyke beard, a gaucho hat and a long black cloak, he worked as British Columbia's travelling judge for 12 years starting in 1858. Begbie travelled all over B.C. on horseback and on foot, using his tent as a judicial chamber during the day. Incidents of violence and highway robbery were rare in B.C., a fact that is often attributed to Begbie's firmness. ♦

it hosts one of Canada's oldest continuous events: the annual ball and parade. Originally designed to help new arrivals feel more comfortable in their new land, the full-dress formal ball has been held for 140 successive years. The early annual ball saw guests arrive by coach and on horseback from as far away as San Francisco and Chicago. They dined and danced at the Clinton Hotel, the biggest and best hotel on the Cariboo Road.

Clinton Country Jamboree
- Reg Conn Centennial Park
- late August

The all-day jamboree consists of exhibitions of arts and crafts plus sales, a pie-baking contest, logger sports and demonstrations of such country skills as roping, gold panning, horseshoes, square dancing and packhorse skills.

Clinton and District Agricultural Society Rodeo
- last weekend of May

Held the weekend following the ball, this traditional rodeo also has a dance on Saturday night, although not so formal.

Farmers' Market
- Bethel Pentecostal Church

Local produce is available on Fridays from 10 a.m. to 2 p.m. between May and October.

Hang-gliding
- Lime Mountain

At nearby Lime Mountain the conditions for hang-gliding are said to be among the best in North America. Hang-glider clubs meet in Clinton in spring and summer, and championships are held in May.

100 MILE HOUSE >>> *population: 1,800*

The origins of 100 Mile House go back to the fur trade, but the town acquired its name during the Cariboo gold rush. It was located 100 miles along the gold-rush trail, which started at Lillooet, the most northerly navigable point on the Fraser River. The community actually originated in the mid-1800s at the junction of Bridge Creek and Little Bridge Creek, a favourite resting place and watering hole for fur traders.

<<< Picturesque countryside surrounds 100 Mile House.

This busy community, tucked among several lakes, offers a good assortment of attractions and activities. The tourist information centre on the west side of Highway 97 can be identified by a pair of Bunyanesque skis that point skyward. "Biggest cross-country skis on the planet" is the claim.

Centennial Park has hiking and biking trails, tennis courts, a pond, playground and ball field. A particularly nice walk leads to the Bridge Creek falls, which do not plunge like Niagara, but are picturesquely spread out in bridal-veil fashion, a popular style with waterfalls these days.

Attractions

• 108 Mile Heritage Site

The biggest log barn in Canada is the centrepiece of this excellent (and free) historical attraction. No one at the site knew where Canada's second-biggest barn was, or where even bigger ones were

that prevented this from being the world's biggest log barn. If this four-tree-long structure was in California, you'd see bumper stickers proclaiming, "We got lost in the biggest log barn in the universe" and T-shirts blaring, "I survived the world's biggest log barn."

The barn dates from 1908 and once housed Clydesdale horses so it had to be big. You can also explore a blacksmith shop, log schoolhouse, ranch house, telegraph office, log cabin, gift shop and 1867 roadhouse. The site is extensive and the roadhouse has been restored with care and expertise. Guides are on hand to provide information and answer questions.

>>> Clydesdale Barn was built for size, not comfort.

83 Mile House Farm Equipment Museum

• Mile 83, Highway 97
• 250-395-3720

This unpretentious spread of pioneer farm equipment is on the west side of 97, 21 kilometres (17 miles) south of 100 Mile House. The farm equipment museum is really a one-man show and the proprietor, Ray Young, is delighted to guide you through his collection of horse-drawn wagons, sleighs, planters, plows, machinery and household gadgets that date from the 1850s through the 1930s. Donations welcome but not required.

As you drive onto the farm you are on the original Cariboo Wagon Road, but you can't go too far unless you walk or bike because there is a bridge that may or may not support an automobile. If you want to drive the original road at a safer spot, Ray will provide exact directions. Roughly: from the museum go south on 97, turn right on Bullock Lake Road and then left on the dirt road at the first intersection.

This dirt road is the wagon road and it reconnects with 97 at an unnamed junction less than 10 kilometres (6 miles) farther south. The road is rough, but quite passable in dry weather.

Imagine, if you will, being on the stage heading south with your satchels full of gold. Out front, 16 clopping

<<< Ray Young is proud of his farm equipment.

hooves are sending up clouds of dust and inside the flies are everywhere. Mosquitoes bite every bit of exposed skin, the temperature is suffocatingly hot and the bouncing coach has forced the smelly old miner opposite you to hurl his breakfast of bacon, beans and coffee. Those were the good old days when men and women were tough.

Stagecoach at the Red Coach Inn

• Highway 97 N.

Towards the rear of the Red Coach Inn, located on the west side of 97 at the north end of town, is a rare surviving stagecoach of the BX Line (Barnard Express and Stage Line, also known as the B.C. Express). Coach number 14 ran between Ashcroft and Prince George and was still in service in 1917, which shows how late the automobile made its presence

<<< Original BX stagecoach on display.

felt on this part of the continent. The barn across the road from the Red Coach Inn was built about 1905 and stabled 50 horses for travellers.

Events
Back to the '50s Show and Shine

• Birch Avenue
• mid-July

Taking the Stagecoach

With the building of dirt roads in the west, the stage had been set (sorry, bad pun) for the B.C. Express Company, known as the BX, to begin operation of what at one time was the longest stagecoach line in North America. Founded in 1862 as Barnard Express and Stage Line, the company hauled mail, passengers and freight along the Cariboo Road between Yale and Barkerville and eventually controlled most of the traffic between the coast and the Cariboo.

The distinctive red-and-yellow stages were a familiar sight on the road until they started to be phased out by motor transport after 1910. By 1920 the company had lost its mail and freight contracts to competitors and soon went out of business. BX coaches can be seen at the Red Coach Inn at 100 Mile House, at Hat Creek Ranch near Cache Creek (where visitors can take a ride) and at O'Keefe Ranch near Vernon.

Riding the Stage

We have all seen western movies in which clean-cut cowboys and pretty young ladies ride spanking clean stagecoaches. Reality was quite different. Sixteen hooves plus four wheels atop a dirt track in an arid land churned up huge clouds of dust that overwhelmed coach and passengers. To avoid the dust, curtains were pulled across the open windows; in the summer the ride was stiflingly hot and in winter there was little to block the frigid air (although dust was not as much of a problem).

Flies are attracted to horses, and clouds of them followed the coaches and worked their way inside to bite and annoy the passengers. Other sources of discomfort were the rutted roads and bouncy springs without shock absorbers. The coach bobbed

Close to 100 vintage cars line up on Birch Avenue with music, food, draws and other activities. Local car buffs also bring their classics to the local A&W on alternate Thursday evenings.

Dogsled Race

- Hills Health and Guest Ranch
- early January

The Jack Gawthorn Memorial Dogsled Race is an exciting event in the depth of winter, held at 108 Mile Ranch.

Farmers' Market

- Donex parking lot
- Fridays

South Cariboo Farmers' Market runs Fridays, in season, from 8:30 a.m. to early afternoon.

Rotary Fall Fair

- South Cariboo Recreation Complex and the Arena
- second weekend in September

Highlights include amusements, business exhibits, farm produce, competitions, local clubs and entertainment.

Rough Stock Rodeo

- Airport Road
- May long weekend

The Little Britches Rodeo for juniors runs at the same time so young and adult get equal billing.

South Cariboo Garlic Festival

- Kariboo Farms, Forest Grove
- mid-August weekend

Plenty of garlic vendors gladly provide samples and organize games and entertainment. A garlic-eating contest is an advertised highlight although it didn't happen on our visit.

Western Week

- South Cariboo Recreation Centre
- week before the May long weekend

Amusement park, street fest, bed races, parade and jail 'n bail keep everyone happy.

On the Road to Williams Lake

Past 108 Mile Heritage Site and the lake behind it, you come upon Lac La Hache, a vacation area 25 kilometres (16 miles) north of 100 Mile House. There are two versions of how the lake and the community got their name. One is the story of a packhorse that fell into the lake and drowned with a cargo of axe heads; the other story has a canoe full of axes tipping over. Axe Lake is the English translation of the French name. The biggest winter attraction in this area is Mount Timothy ski hill, serviced by a triple chairlift. The hill is 23 kilometres (14 miles) east of Lac La Hache.

Heading north from Lac La Hache the valley widens into rolling ranchland and the hills flatten to mere humps on the horizon. Like 70 Mile House, 150 Mile House is but a flash of a few sleep 'n'eats before your arrival at the spectacularly scenic entry to Williams Lake. The town appears at the end of a long lake framed by steeper, higher hills. On late afternoons the sun dances over the lake and sets beside or behind the town, depending on the season. As you might expect, the lake is also called Williams Lake (also without an apostrophe).

 WILLIAMS LAKE >>> *population: 12,000*

The town of Williams Lake has a distinction that only the readers of this book are likely to be aware of—it is approximately the midpoint of Highway 97. Hard to believe, but it is 1,640 kilometres (1,020

along like a rowboat on a stormy sea, and it was quite common for passengers to lean out the window, amid the flies and dust, and throw up a greasy roadhouse breakfast.

In a historical account written for the *Kelowna Daily Courier* in 1962, Art Gray wrote: "In 1912 even the main Okanagan highway was pretty rugged travelling ... The side roads used to consist of two ruts filled to the brim with powdery dust. The main roads had four ruts, more traffic and more dust. In summer it was a long dusty strip bereft of shade and in winter the piercing north winds blew right through you. In spring it was a quagmire with a series of bog holes into which gravel dumped by the public works just sank out of sight." Gray concluded, "In writing these stories of the old days nostalgia may overcome me at times, but not when I think of the roads. 1912 roads ... brother you can have 'em!"

At Hat Creek Ranch near Cache Creek, I rode one of the stages of the BX line pulled by two stout horses, and I can confirm two discomforts: flies and heat. Yes, flies do love horses, and while the coaches have open windows, the horses' gaits are insufficiently fast to create a breeze, so ventilation is nil. In summer the temperature soars both inside and out. Yet the ride on the smooth roads at Hat Creek was quite comfortable and a long way from inducing nausea, so I heartily recommend stopping in for a ride.

Another cinematic fantasy is the robbing of stagecoaches by masked men. Although the coaches from Barkerville often carried chests of gold worth up to $600,000 during a time when a man might earn $10 a day, robberies

continued on following page

were infrequent. In fact, the practice of hiring armed guards to protect the booty was soon abandoned because they were not needed. The first recorded holdup occurred in 1885, after 20 years of successfully delivered gold shipments, when two highwaymen made off with $4,000 near 82 Mile House. The last holdup, and reportedly the last robbery of a stagecoach in North America, took place in November 1909. The robbers, a man and a woman who had gained a small amount of money, were soon arrested. Their guilt could not be proven, so they were simply put on a train and sent out of the country. ♦

miles) south to Weed, California, and about the same distance north to the Yukon border.

The town is bright, clean and prosperous looking. Having recently celebrated its 75th birthday, it hasn't had much time to get rundown and ugly, although age isn't always a criterion as some settlements start out rundown and ugly and stay that way.

In the summer, Williams Lake's first major intersection as you arrive from the south is planted with roses, marigolds and other flora that the hurried motorist may not appreciate unless a red light or a flat tire gives cause to pause. Look around and smell the roses.

Attractions
Kiwanis Park
• downtown next to recreation complex

Amenities include tennis courts, gardens, a wading pool and picnic area, plus an ice skating rink nearby.

Boitanio Park
• downtown

Summer concerts on Thursday evenings feature visiting and local performers. The shows start at 6 p.m. The 17-hectare (42-acre) park features 2.5 kilometres (1.5 miles) of pathways meandering through rose gardens, forests, picnic areas and a play area.

Museum of the Cariboo-Chilcotin

- 113 N. 4th Avenue
- 250-392-7404

Puttering around this pretty museum is a great way to learn about local gold mining history. It has a distinctly western flair, being the site of the B.C. Cowboy Hall of Fame. The museum is billed as B.C.'s only ranch and rodeo museum and who could argue against such an exclusive promotion. Across the street, a 1947 pumper truck is displayed at the fire hall.

Scout Island

- north end of lake

Just west of 97 at the north end of Williams Lake lies Scout Island, which is actually two small islands connected by footbridges, and a natural sanctuary with walking trails, viewing areas, a beach, boat launch and a nature centre in a log cabin. This end of the lake is on the flight path of hundreds of bird species that migrate from as far south as Peru and Chile and, after a rest at Williams Lake, continue on to the Northwest Territories and Alaska. White pelicans, swans, eagles and numerous species of duck have been spotted. Fox, beaver and otter live in the area. In winter this is an excellent skating area.

Station House Gallery

- 1 N. Mackenzie Avenue

Constructed in 1919 for the Pacific Great Eastern Railway, the building is as old as they get in Williams Lake. Once a train station, it is now an art gallery with displays by local artists.

Xats'ull Heritage Village

- 3405 Mountain House Road
- 250-297-6502

This Native village beside the Fraser River recreates the traditional way of life. Daily tours and extended

The Roadhouse Murder Mystery

The most interesting story perpetuated at 108 Mile Heritage Site is the tale of a Scottish woman by the name of Agnus MacVee, who went on a killing spree and may have murdered as many as 50 miners in the 1870s. The following unverified information is from printed sheets given out at the 108 Mile Heritage Site.

Agnus MacVee, with her husband Jim and son-in-law Al Riley, ran the 108 Hotel and supplied liquor and women to the lonely miners. In 1875 Henry Dawson arrived at the hotel with $11,000 in gold. Al Riley later told authorities he had found Dawson's horse running loose and a search found the semi-submerged, battered body of Dawson, who had been shot in the back and apparently dumped in the lake.

Murder number one. Because subsequent victims were far from home and out of touch with family and friends, many missing persons went unnoticed and the deaths were not immediately reported. However, a few years later, one of the victims turned out to be Agnus's husband, Jim. The police investigated the poisoning of Jim, and though Al Riley implicated Agnus, he was the one they executed. Agnus managed to smuggle some poison into the Kamloops jail and later took her own life.

Caches of gold and gold coins have been uncovered in farmers' fields and elsewhere in the area. Are these the treasures that Agnus hid after she murdered their rightful owners? ♦

stays are available. Subjects of study include the Shuswap language, heritage arts and crafts, preparation of traditional feasts, plants, wildlife, songs, dances, traditional lands, the gold-rush trail and rituals.

Events
Harvest Fair
- Stampede Grounds
- second weekend of September

A traditional fall fair that features fun festivities for fanatics from age four to five score. Included are a logging show, lumberjack competition, horse show, pet parade, musicians, storytellers, livestock show and competitions in such diverse skills as knitting, quilting, wine making and growing apples and onions.

Powwow
- Highway 97
- mid-June

South of Williams Lake on Highway 97, the Chief Wil-Yum RV Park hosts a powwow on the Fathers' Day weekend.

Williams Lake Stampede
- Stampede Grounds
- first weekend in July

Just north of Scout Island nature preserve is a huge event—the annual stampede. The Williams Lake Stampede is one of the biggest rodeos in British Columbia and the biggest event of the year in this part of the province.

Visitor Info
- 1148 S. Broadway
- 250-392-5025
- www.landwithoutlimits.com

 DETOUR >>> **TO THE COAST**
Highway 20, a.k.a. the Chilcotin Highway, intersects Highway 97 and is one of surprisingly few roads linking mainland British Columbia to the Pacific Ocean. It also provides access to Tweedsmuir Provincial Park and the settlement of Bella Coola. From Williams Lake this is a

great route from which to get a taste of the absolute vastness of the western Canadian wilderness. Another such sampling awaits us north of Fort Nelson on Highway 97.

Bella Coola is 455 kilometres (285 miles) west of Williams Lake at the end of a long, saltwater fjord that is part of the Pacific Ocean. The Bella Coola valley provided an alternate access route to the Cariboo goldfields in 1858 and it was the location of a Hudson's Bay trading post in 1867. The town was also home to Norwegian colonists from Minnesota who settled because the landscape reminded them of their Scandinavian homeland.

The snakelike path of Highway 20 includes The Hill, which makes the final descent at an exciting 18 percent drop, to its terminus at Bella Coola. The highway, also named the Freedom Road, was opened in 1953 when the citizens of Bella Coola demanded a non-ferry connection to the rest of the province and started building it themselves.

From Bella Coola a passenger boat connects to northern Vancouver Island to make an interesting, but lengthy (in time as much as distance) alternative to returning via 97. Another choice is to take Highway 20 about half way, sample the wilderness, stay overnight (or longer) at Clearwater Lake Lodge and Resort (250-476-1150) and then make your return to Highway 97.

Located just past Kleena Kleena, the Clearwater Lodge provides campsites, cabins, canoes, rooms and meals. An interesting outing from the lodge is to take Miner Road south off Highway 20 from a point about 10 kilometres (6 miles) east of the lodge. This road leads to an old gold mine up in the mountains, but along the way you get to experience the almost infinite vastness of the untouched Chilcotin territory as well as its total silence. The cry of a crow, the outburst of an osprey or the whoosh of flapping wings is all that one is likely to hear (turn off that CD player).

Once you are on Miner Road turn left at the first fork and then stop between two lakes that have yet to be named. At the next fork you can turn right to Miner Lake or take the left fork and then the next left fork to forge on into the wilderness. There are more forks to be navigated, but I don't remember them. Besides, you will probably get lost if you follow my directions, and that isn't a good thing, so get a local to spell it out for you.

Halfway between Williams Lake and Prince George, Quesnel greets the traveller who arrives from the south with welcoming parks, flowers, green space, murals and an interesting information station/museum with picnic tables, washrooms and lots of summer greenery.

The northbound exit from the town is also interesting, albeit in a much different way. The economy of Quesnel is based on the forest industry, and the industrial area adjacent to the highway is a cluster of mills. About 50 metres (150 feet) east of 97, a viewing stand offers a panoramic eyescape of smokestacks and stacks of lumber. Viewing stands of this type are usually reserved for the splendours of nature so give credit to Quesnel for opening up the heart of its manufacturing community for all to see. Tours of the wood-products factories are conducted regularly. Check times by calling 250-992-8716.

By the way, if you don't want to be tagged as a tourist, don't pronounce the "s" in the town's name. Say "Quen*nel*." The name was borrowed from Jules Quesnelle, a lieutenant in Simon Fraser's expedition of exploration. Originally the town was known as Quesnelle Mouth, the spot where the Quesnel River flows into the Fraser River.

Quesnel boomed in the late 1800s with the discovery of gold in the area and was the service centre where prospectors stocked up with supplies before heading east to gold towns such as Williams Creek and

>>> What better welcoming sign to celebrate gold mining?

<<< A viewing stand facilitates observing the lumber industry.

Barkerville, the centre of the great Cariboo gold rush. Quesnel is still the gateway to these historic communities.

Between the contrasting focal points of the town entrance and exit lies a clean and vibrant community with a pretty downtown that sports a variety of shops and lots of flowers and friendly people. The tourism office booklet entitled *An Historic Walking Tour* suggests a pedestrian route through town that will appeal to history and nostalgia buffs.

Attractions
Antique Machinery Park
• on Highway 97, 11 kilometres (7 miles) south of Quesnel

For those with an interest in technology from the early 1800s through to the 1950s, this is another of the many worthwhile stops on 97 that specialize in metal things that make smoke and noise. Four main categories of machines are exhibited: mining, forestry, transportation and agriculture. The exhibits have been restored to their original condition with several pieces of working machinery. Hours are irregular as volunteers staff the park.

Heritage Walk
• downtown

Pick up a copy of the historic-walk brochure and take the self-guided tour through town. At Heritage Corner (Front Street and Carson Avenue) you will find a Cornish water wheel that was once used in

>>> Heritage Corner has links for four important events.

mining, the 1929 bridge across the Fraser, a cairn commemorating the Collins Overland Telegraph link from New Westminster in 1865 and the remains of the steamer *Enterprise*.

The bridge crossing the raging Fraser River is now for foot traffic only and is the start of the Riverfront Trail Park for walking, hiking and biking. Across the street from Heritage Corner stands an original 1862 log Hudson's Bay store that now houses a souvenir shop. Near the site two heritage buildings, the Quesnel and Cariboo hotels, have been restored to replicate the era when they housed gold miners on their way to and from various discoveries.

>>> Souvenirs are sold at the 1862 Hudson's Bay Store.

LeBourdais Park

• at the tourist info centre on Highway 97, south end of town

Most fairs and festivals in Quesnel take place in this park. Its features include a water park for the kids, a museum, a huge grass playing field, gardens and a big, bright mural. Nearby you will find tennis courts, a ball field, rose gardens and a historic cemetery. The tower on the front lawn holds a 180-kilogram (400-pound) bell that was previously used by the fire department.

Quesnel and District Museum

- 410 Kinchant Street
- 250-992-9580

Local history is the focus of the museum, which is located beside the tourist info station. Of special interest is a display showing the contributions of the Chinese who came to this area.

<<< The museum is conveniently located beside the tourist info centre.

Quesnel Lake

- 60 kilometres east of Highway 97

A body of water is not normally an attraction in a land that is puddled with aquatic recreation. This one, however, is dubbed "World's Deepest Fjord Lake." A fjord lake is one that has been carved by a glacier and Quesnel Lake is said to be 530 metres (1,739 feet) deep. Although not particularly large, it is in the shape of a wishbone with three arms and many bays. This form creates 800 kilometres (500 miles) of shoreline.

Riverfront Trail

Nearly the entire pathway that runs alongside the Fraser River and the North Quesnel River is paved and the 9 kilometres (5 miles) are perfect for a walk, run, bike ride or roller blade. Or you can do it on a horse and let the beast get the exercise. There is plenty of history along the way.

Events
Billy Barker Days
- various locations
- third weekend in July

B.C.'s third largest outdoor family festival squeezes 150 events into 4 days, including raft races on the Fraser River, street music, a parade, fireworks, car racing, stage shows, pie eating, watermelon seed spitting and the Quesnel Rodeo, the largest amateur rodeo in the province.

Bluegrass music jamboree
- Seniors' Centre, 461 Carson Avenue
- late April
- 250-992-3991

Where The Rivers Meet bluegrass jamboree has been going on for a decade with four days of down-home music.

Cariboo Highland Games
- LeBourdais Park and Twin Arena
- mid June

Scottish-themed events include the caber toss, haggis hurl, sheaf toss, frying pan toss, truck pull, ceilidh and Scottish trivia contest. The Scotch-tasting competition is followed by the Scotch boat race, a challenging combination.

Visitor Info
- 703 Carson Avenue
- 250-992-8716, 800-992-4922
- www.northcariboo.com/visitorservices

26 DETOUR >>> **THE ROAD TO BILLY BARKER'S GOLD**

East of Quesnel you will encounter one of the most desirable detours on all of 97. Highway 26 leads directly to the motherlode of gold-rush lore, and to the reason for the existence of this portion of Highway 97 and many of the communities along it.

Highway 26 opened in 1967 to provide better access to the communities of Wells and Barkerville, 75 and 82 kilometres (47 and 51 miles), respectively, east of Quesnel. The original gold-rush road, the Cariboo Wagon Road, approached Barkerville in a circuitous fashion and entered the town from the opposite direction.

Cottonwood House Historic Site

- 4660 Barkerville Highway
- 250-992-2071

Just 20 minutes from Quesnel, Cottonwood House is an interesting stop of historic interest on the way to Barkerville and an excellent place to whet your appetite for the gold-rush city ahead. This was the first overnight stop for the stagecoach that left Quesnel on the three-day journey to Barkerville. The 1864 buildings are intact and include the roadhouse, a guest cabin, barn, root cellar and outbuildings. The original wagon road runs right by the front door of the roadhouse. Luggage carried on top of the stages was unloaded directly through a second-floor doorway.

While the house is large, it is still difficult to imagine it filled with a dozen overnight guests, a maid, two cooks, plus the owner, his wife, their 12 children and their governess. Tours of the house are conducted either on schedule or on demand and visitors are free to wander the grounds and ask questions of the student staff. The heritage site is run by the local school board as a Career Programs Youth Project. It offers cabin accommodation for $35, which includes breakfast and admission to the grounds for two, or a camping spot with admission for two and breakfast for $15. Amazing bargains, as a single admission is $4.50.

<<< Cottonwood House sits on the Cariboo Wagon Road.

Cottonwood Trading Post

Just a couple of kilometres past Cottonwood House, the Cottonwood Trading Post has a very small and specialized museum dedicated to the

Roadhouses

The establishment of B.C.'s early roadhouses is also the story of the development of hotels and motels in the west. At first these primitive overnight stops were called restaurants until the more appropriate title roadhouse came into use.

The pack trains that travelled north through the Cariboo only covered about 10 kilometres (6 miles) a day, a pace that created the need (and opportunity) for frequent food and lodging stops. Roadhouses began to appear within a few miles of each other. When better trails were constructed, laden horses covered 25 or more kilometres (16 miles) per day. Where the land was open, easily travelled, and water and meadow were available, the density of roadhouses increased. This type of terrain, such as the ranchland between Cache Creek and Quesnel, was settled early and many housewives earned a steady income by feeding and housing travellers.

The first wayside houses were crude log shacks with a small dirt-floored room. A stone fireplace at one end served for cooking, heating and light. The unwashed "guests" slept on the floor while the owner slept on top of a wood counter that harboured the liquor supply. The selling of alcohol, at 25 cents a shot, was a major income producer.

Many prospectors preferred sleeping outdoors to being squeezed in beside unwashed bodies that were home to lice, fleas and bedbugs. The parasites were impossible to get rid of under the crowded, unsanitary conditions; rare was the roadhouse that was not infested. In some instances two or three men, strangers to each other, were shoehorned into a bed for the night. A tin bath was provided with a charge of about 5 cents for warm,

>>> The snowmobile museum caters to special interests.

snowmobile, not to be missed if you have affection for the noisy, powered snow runners. Also not to be missed, if you are in the area on a Saturday night, is an old-fashioned jam session featuring real cowboys and other locals strumming guitars and singing country songs. Their music is unexpectedly excellent. The rickety canopy beside the trading post shelters the singers while bonfires keep the audience warm.

WELLS >>> population: 250

Wells is a small mountain community just outside Barkerville and it has a dual identity as a bedroom community for those who work in Barkerville and as a colony for struggling artists. The community has some colourful shops and studios, but the numbers of Closed and For Sale signs indicate that business is marginal.

In 1927, Fred Wells discovered a vein of gold-bearing quartz and the townsite was subsequently founded. Wells became a thriving company town with numerous recreational facilities that attracted miners, their families and independent businesses. By the early 1940s, the population had grown to 4,500, making Wells, for a short time, the largest town in the Cariboo.

The big Wells Museum (250-994-3422) on the main road showcases mining displays and memorabilia from the glory days. Exhibits relate to the second Cariboo gold rush, which took place between 1930 and 1967, and the building of Wells. The yellow museum building used to be the offices of Island Mountain Mine.

<<< The big yellow Wells Museum is hard to miss.

 **BARKERVILLE**

The entire town of Barkerville is a government historic site and a major tourist attraction. Some of the buildings date back to the mid-1860s but most fall within a slightly later time period. Barkerville requires at least one full day of exploration. The drive from Quesnel takes an hour with another hour spent exploring places between, so leave early. And dress warmly with an eye to the weather. This is a mountain town where it rains more often than not in summer and buildings have to be heated most days of the year.

The best thing about Barkerville is its authenticity. The doctor's office is real, as is the newspaper office and the bakery and the saloon. Town characters roam the streets to give lectures, perform skits, sing and dance, and before long you will almost believe they are real too. If you go into a house you might find a woman in a long dress and bonnet cooking in the kitchen. She will be using ingredients

clean water. As more men used the water the price went down and by the end of the week the cost for the use of tepid, dirty water was 1 cent.

Overnighting at the Yale roadhouse, near the start of the Cariboo Wagon Road, was hardly a holiday affair. One guest described his stay this way: "There is but one public eating house in the town, and invariably the diet is bacon, salmon, bread, tea and coffee ... the charge is $1.00 a meal. No milk or butter is ever seen. It is ... a miserable log hut partly barked over, and with a dirt floor. Everything is done in the same room—which is no more than 12' x 14' and consequently cramped for space, and hot as an oven. At night miners sleep on the floor." The supply of food was dependent on pack-train delivery and at 50 cents a pound for freight, it was expensive. Fresh produce was rare.

In the goldfields, entertainment became a part of the roadhouse experience. Hand organs, pianos and billiard tables came all the way from San Francisco by boat and on the backs of mules. Prostitutes also came, as did gamblers, tricksters, hucksters and others whose intention was to separate the few wealthy miners from their money.

Fire was the dreaded enemy of the roadhouses, and although great caution was taken, sparks from the chimney frequently ignited the dry, wooden shake roofs. Few of the old log buildings remain today and indeed most of the original town of Barkerville was burned to the ground in 1869. The residents began the task of rebuilding their town the next day. ◆

The Reason for Canada?

The actors/historians who give tours through Barkerville make a case for the mining town being the most important community in the Dominion of Canada. Their reasoning goes like this:

> When gold was discovered in 1862 there was no Canada.

> The mined gold was so weighty and so valuable that a road was needed to get it out, not to get supplies in, as is usually reported. Thus the Cariboo Wagon Road was built.

> With a population of 33,000, Barkerville was bigger than Vancouver and Victoria, and while it had little political clout, it did have economic power.

> Products arriving from eastern North America and Europe were excessively expensive in the west because of the distance they had to travel by ocean.

> The eastern provinces united to become Canada in 1867, and when B.C. was later invited to join Confederation, its most important asset was gold. A condition for joining the Dominion was that a rail line be built across the country so goods could get to the people of Barkerville more quickly and more cheaply than by ship.

> Agreement was reached; Canada expanded to the Pacific on July 20, 1871, with the addition of British Columbia to Confederation, and it was the gold in Barkerville that was the key. ♦

available before 1900 and will assume the role of a maid or housewife and gladly talk about her life in the 1860s or 1870s. She will probably offer you a sample of her cooking if your timing is good.

Barkerville's two long streets and hundred or so buildings beg to be explored and savoured. Be sure to visit the buildings that make up Chinatown. Close to half of the population of Barkerville was Chinese, many of them merchants who lived in the better part of town. One admission fee covers everything except horse-drawn wagon rides, gold panning and performances at the Theatre Royal.

>>> A blacksmith chats with a customer.

>>> But for the tourists, this could be 1870.

Billy Barker

The inspiration for the town of Barkerville came from William (Billy) Barker, who was born in England, but left in his mid-20s to join the rush for gold in California. Barker arrived in British Columbia in 1858 during the Fraser River gold rush. Like many others, he worked his way up the rivers and eventually began to work Williams Creek, above present-day Barkerville.

The historic Barker No. 2 claim was registered on August 17, 1862. Most people felt Barker was foolish to stake a claim so far down the creek, but in their search for gold, Barker and his group dug deeper shafts than any others in the area. After two futile attempts they found rich gold deposits at a depth of 13 metres (40 feet). From this depth down to bedrock at 17 metres (52 feet), the yield was incredible. His claims, 270 by 33 metres (800 by 100 feet), eventually yielded about 37,500 ounces (1,100 kilograms) of gold.

Barker took his newfound wealth to mild Victoria to enjoy a comfortable winter and there married Elizabeth Collyer, who had recently arrived from London. In the summer of 1863 she accompanied her new husband to Williams Creek, where a boomtown, soon to be known as Barkerville, was springing up around other rich strikes. After a successful mining season operating three shafts, the couple returned to Victoria.

Barker sold his shares in the claim that made him famous, Elizabeth died in 1865 at age 38, and his fortunes began to decline. None of his subsequent ventures paid off. Dying from cancer of the jaw, he took refuge in the Old Men's Home in Victoria where he died in 1894 and was buried in an unmarked pauper's grave. ◆

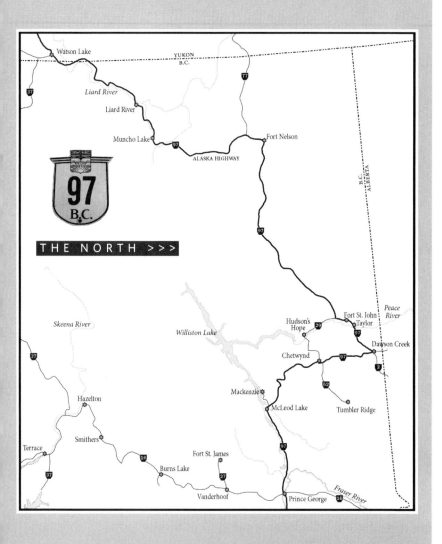

CHAPTER FIVE

The North

THE ODD THING ABOUT PRINCE GEORGE IS THAT PEOPLE IN THE SOUTH PERCEIVE
it as being in the north and on the edge of civilization. Actually, it is
close to the geographic centre of B.C. and north of it there is plenty
of life, activity and sightseeing. This skewed view of Canadian geography
is common west of the Maritimes, where the vast majority of
the population lives in the southern third of each province. The northern
two-thirds are so desolate and deserted that people who venture
as far as the middle feel that they have reached the Far North. Those
plucky individuals who choose to live in and explore the real north
know better.

PRINCE GEORGE >>> population: 76,000

The biggest city in central and northern British Columbia is located
just 118 kilometres (70 miles) north of Quesnel. It was founded by
Simon Fraser in 1807 as a fur-trading post near the junction of the
Fraser River and its tributary, the Nechako River. The name Prince
George was chosen to honour the 13-year-old son of the English king,
George V.

Significant growth didn't start until a century ago, when it was
rumoured that the Grand Trunk Pacific Railway (now CN) would pass
near the fur post, as it eventually did in 1914. Another growth spurt in
the 1950s occurred when pulp mills and sawmills became major

175

operations. The city has continued to grow and now contains a university, museums, several art galleries and a symphony orchestra. But in many ways Prince George is still a frontier town teetering on the brink between the domesticated, predictable south and the feral, unaccountable north. While patrons of the arts pursue their pleasures, some interesting characters prowl the downtown streets. These marginalized individuals seem to connect the city to the atmosphere of the western frontier days.

The cultural contrast is most obvious when you visit the new civic centre, off Patricia Boulevard, with its spectacular, if somewhat sterile, architecture. The Two Rivers Gallery, library, fountains, swimming pools and clock tower are avant-garde. Then walk over to 2nd or 3rd Avenue, where pawnshops and junk shops sit in proximity to various drinking establishments. Many of the bars are old-style hotels with two or three floors of rooms above the drinking area. Many of their patrons wear cowboy hats and boots, but their transport of choice is now the pickup truck rather than the horse.

Prince George's huge downtown seems to be about twice the size of downtown Kelowna, Highway 97's biggest city. Several large, modern hotels anchor the downtown landscape and draw tourists and other visitors to the city centre. This is a good thing. The outlying commercial strips and shopping districts are somewhat separated from the heart of the city and seem less important to commerce than is usually the case.

Attractions
Farmers' Market
- George and Third streets
- Saturday mornings, May through September

Held downtown at the Courthouse Plaza, the market features products from farmers, bakers, artisans and crafters. Entertainers often add to the market's atmosphere.

Ferguson Lake
Ferguson Lake nature reserve, 25 minutes north of downtown, protects the exceptionally rich plant and animal life in the area. No motorboats are allowed, but canoes and kayaks are welcome. A 3-kilometre (2-mile) hiking trail circles the lake.

Forests for the World

• Cranbrook Hill and Kueng Road

Don't let the name conjure visions of palm, eucalyptus and teak. Rather, Forests for the World is a peaceful oasis of native trees, conveniently close to the city. A 10-minute walk from the parking lot, Shane Lake is a tranquil, forest watershed environment. To further appreciate some of the forests and mountains that surround Prince George take a 15-minute walk up the viewpoint trail to the lookout.

Fort George Park

• off Queensway Street

In addition to the flower gardens, the riverside bike/walk path, the ballpark, tennis courts, bandshell and kids' water park, this big patch of greenery features a steam railway, a tiny historic rail station, an old schoolhouse, a museum and a children's exploration centre. There is a full day of family fun here.

The 1912 steam train runs from noon to 4 p.m. on summer weekends and holidays. The little 0-4-0 "dinkey" engine pulls passenger cars along a .62 kilometre (.5 mile) track. A seat on the train goes for the old-fashioned price of one dollar.

<<< Prince George's "dinkey" steam engine pulls passenger cars.

Fraser–Fort George Regional Museum

• 333 Becott Place
• 250-562-1612

Entering this modern museum is confusing because the laughter of children belies the serious business of history. The museum shares space with a hall of fame, which shares space with a simulated ride theatre, and none of these areas have a distinct entrance or exit. The laughing children are enjoying Exploration Place, where many of the hands-on exhibits are designed for children. The kids can dig for dinosaur bones, hold a hissing cockroach and play on a sternwheeler. On our visit we almost stumbled over two large turtles ambling across the floor with a three-year-old in hot pursuit.

The museum portion isn't as much fun for adults, although there are excellent displays of the area's early days with a typical frontier store and loads of artifacts. The local sports hall of fame is in the museum building as is the Virtual Voyages Theatre motion pods that simulate action adventures.

Hiking and Biking

There are more than 120 parks within the city limits of Prince George, so finding a spot of greenery for a rest, meditation, ride, walk or picnic is never a problem. An extensive trail system runs beside the rivers. The 12-kilometre (8-mile) Heritage River Trail wanders from John Hart Bridge to Cottonwood Island and through Fort George Park and Paddlewheel Park. The circular, crushed-gravel trail provides some interesting angles from which to view the city. A trail map is available from the tourist office.

Behind the University of Northern B.C. (3333 University Way), the Greenway Trail wanders though impressive scenery and joins the paths in Forests for the World.

Huble Homestead
- Mitchell Road
- 250-563-9225

A living museum, the Huble Homestead, 50 kilometres (29 miles) north of the city off Highway 97, was settled in 1905 by Al Huble. He established a trading post and eventually added several barns, a warehouse and a squared-log house. The nice thing about Huble Homestead is that it is just a plain, old turn-of-the-century ranch and a great place to wander. No thrill rides, no mysteries, no extravaganza. Open May through October with guides on the site daily.

Park Drive-In theatre

• 9660 Raceway Road

• 250-967-4342

Just north of the city off Highway 97 sits the Park Drive-In. This relic from before the days of home theatre and multiplex cinemas is one of two outdoor cinemas on British Columbia's Highway 97. The other is near Enderby, just north of the Okanagan.

Prince George Native Art Gallery

1600 3rd Avenue

250-614-7726

A wide range of arts and crafts from across B.C. illustrates First Nations' history through art interpretation. You'll find carvings, limited edition prints, custom framing, handcrafted jewellery and Native literature here.

Railway and Forestry Museum

• 850 River Road

• 250-563-7351

For the railway buff this is heaven on Earth, with dozens of trains in various states of restoration, an enormous wooden snowplow, an electric engine, a steam engine, cabooses, sleeper cars, an authentic old station, a re-created new one and a miniature railway that weaves through the train displays. The total comes to 60 pieces of rolling stock, nine historic buildings and numerous smaller bits on a 3-hectare (8-acre) site.

<<< Train buffs will appreciate the Prince George Railway Museum.

You will also discover handcars, a little house that displays the history of the telephone, a building that shows the work of Ukrainian settlers and much more. If you love old railways, plan to stay for the day. The forestry part of the museum is barely noticeable in all the excitement. On the first weekend of October, Harry Potter takes over the train museum and children and adults enjoy a spooky good time. Highlights are rides on the Hogwarts Express, Hogwarts classes (potions, charms, herbology, etc.) and a walk through the haunted prison.

Rainbow Park
• Rainbow Drive and Ospika Boulevard

This park features the best flower gardens in the city plus a playground, picnic shelter and walking trails. It's a favourite for special-occasion photographs and it has a great winter sledding hill.

Spruce City Wildlife Fish Hatchery
• River Road
• 250-563-5437

Salmon are raised here in the spring and trout in the summer. The hatchery is housed in a log building on the banks of the Nechako River in Cottonwood Island Nature Park on River Road. Tours are available.

Two Rivers Art Gallery
• 725 Civic Plaza
• 250-614-7800

>>> Civic Plaza sports a clock tower next to the art gallery.

The dramatic architecture of the gallery building can be as interesting as what it contains. The gallery's brochure describes it thus: "The sloping roof, the curved ribs that front the galleria and the forecourt of boulders and shrubs together represent one of the city's most significant natural features—the escarpments along the Nechako and Fraser rivers. Constructed from Douglas fir, the ribs also speak to the importance of the forestry industry in the region. Wood is used throughout the Gallery in places where visitors will experience it most directly." Big, bright rooms with 7-metre (20-foot) ceilings house the gallery exhibits.

Skiing
Hart Highlands Winter Club
• 250-962-8006

This small hill within city limits has 11 machine-groomed runs, rentals, ski school and T-bar lift.

Purden Ski Village
• 60 kilometres (38 miles) east of Prince George on the Yellowhead Highway, then 4 kilometres north
• 250-565-7777

Purden is the largest ski mountain in central British Columbia, with 400 vertical metres (1,200 feet) of skiing on dry powder snow, treed runs and uncrowded slopes.

Tabor Mountain Ski Resort
• Yellowhead Highway, 20 kilometres (12.5 miles) east of Prince George
• 250-963-7542

The downhill skiing area has a 240-metre (800-foot) vertical drop serviced by a triple lift and a T-bar.

Cross-Country Skiing
Prince George also has superb cross-country skiing. There are trails on Cottonwood Island, at the University of Northern B.C. campus, in Forests for the World and at Moore's Meadow. Trails, for a fee, can be found at Otway Ski Trails and Tabor Mountain.

Events

Mennonite Fall Fair

- Civic Centre
- end of September
- 250-963-9276

Fair Trade coffee, baking, crafts, produce, used books, clothes, a silent auction, garage sale and Ten Thousand Villages crafts from around the world are all on site. A traditional Mennonite lunch and snacks are served all day with all proceeds in support of world and local relief.

Ol' Sawmill Bluegrass Jamboree

- mid-August

Held at a site on North Nechako Road, this four-day musical event is for families, with camping, workshops, arts and crafts, play areas and talented performers from Texas to Nova Scotia (as well as northern B.C.).

Prince George Exhibition

- Exhibition Park
- Ospika Boulevard
- mid-August

The exhibition has been held annually since 1906 and features a midway, entertainment and contests that make it something of a combined fall fair, carnival and trade show.

Tourist Info

- 1300 1st Avenue
- 250-562-3700, 800-668-7646
- www.tourismpg.com

On the Road to Chetwynd

The next stretch of 97 is known as the John Hart Highway. The 406-kilometre (250-mile) section begins at Prince George and ends at Dawson Creek. On the map it looks like a long, desolate drive, but it actually is immensely interesting, with changing geography and enough natural features and small settlements to hold your attention. North of Prince George the terrain becomes mountainous and in July there are still a few patches of snow on the loftiest peaks. This is a vast improvement over the rather dull green corridor that links Quesnel and Prince George. I should call it a green-and-brown corridor, because the pine beetle and the spruce budworm are killing the evergreens that shoulder the road and turning them into everbrowns.

Most of the way to Fort St. John, which is just past Dawson Creek, you are travelling in an agricultural valley and the farther north you

<<< Agricultural panoramas extend into northern B.C.

go, the wider the valley gets until it is almost a plain. This is the only prairie in British Columbia, and 90 percent of grain grown in the province comes from this long stretch of arable land. The delightful panoramas keep the eyes wide open.

Some of the wildlife sightings that my wife Lian and I made on one recent trip between Quesnel and Dawson Creek included a bear cub crossing the road, numerous deer with fawns, a mother moose with two calves, a large black bear, a fox and two huge horses crossing a remote section of the highway.

McLeod Lake, about 135 kilometres (83 miles) north of Prince George, is for me a disappointing collection of cabins and a couple of stores that have seen better times. I have a nostalgic connection to McLeod Lake because, as a teen, I hitchhiked west from Toronto and managed to land a summer job there helping to clear a pathway for the Peace River power lines that are visible, from time to time, in the distance. I lived in a trailer and took a helicopter and boat to work in the bush, chopping down small trees with an axe. In the early 1960s the minuscule settlement buzzed with activity.

Keep your eyes open for the junction that leads to Mackenzie, 29 kilometres (18 miles) to the west. A large tourism trailer on Highway 97 provides abundant information about this small community. Outdoor activities and exploration are the main tourist attractions, but Mackenzie is best known for being home to the world's largest tree crusher, which is on display downtown. The 175-ton LeTourneau giant was used to level trees in the valley that was flooded when the W.A.C. Bennett dam was built, and to clear a path for the Peace River power lines. It was designed to put me, with my axe, out of a job, but it didn't perform as well as a squad of men with chainsaws. It often got stuck in the muck.

>>> Bijoux Falls tumbles down beside a pleasant picnic spot.

Mackenzie's museum must have one of the shortest time spans for a historical collection. The town began in 1966 when a power dam created Williston Lake, billed as the largest man-made lake in Canada, so its recorded history is only 40 years. Ask the museum staff to screen the video of the tree crusher in action.

About 25 kilometres past the Mackenzie junction, Bijoux Falls tumbles in three layers of cascades beside a pleasant picnic spot and provincial park. There is but one sign announcing the falls, so scan the road ahead as you drive and prepare for the short turnoff to the west.

Beyond the falls you ascend the Pine Pass Summit at 874 metres (2,867 feet) and cross over the Pine River bridge. Since McLeod Lake, Highway 97 has gradually shifted direction and is now heading more eastwards to Alberta than northwards to the Yukon. This eastward direction continues through Chetwynd to Dawson Creek, where you are nearly at the Alberta border. Then it's northward ho!

CHETWYND >>> population: 3,200

I like towns that have a specialty or a unique feature that they can proclaim to the world. Chetwynd's claim to fame is its collection of wooden sculptures carved by chainsaws. Outside the tourist info stop

on Highway 97 in the centre of town, a number of carvings are lined up beneath the "Welcome to Chetwynd" sign. The town offers a map and a walking tour that will lead you to more of the wooden sculptures. An annual chainsaw carving competition is being planned.

Chetwynd's other main attraction, in the southwest end of town, is an old general store/post office that has been transformed into the Little Prairie Heritage Museum. The collections are small-town routine, but the rural setting is exceptional, with lots of small outbuildings and barns to explore. The custodians are wonderfully friendly.

The town's odd name comes courtesy of Ralph Chetwynd, a former B.C. minister of railways.

Tourist Info
- 5217 North Access Road
- 250-788-1943
- www.gochetwynd.com

DAWSON CREEK >>> *population: 18,500*

The city of Dawson Creek marks Mile Zero of the Alaska Highway, a fact that is recognized by a commemorative signpost in the centre of town and an assortment of Mile Zero campgrounds, restaurants, cairns, motels and more. With such intense competition, Highway 97 pretty much fades into oblivion here, except for the provincial road

Alaska Highway

The most recent and best-documented part of Highway 97 is the Alaska Highway. During the Second World War, the United States wanted an inland military route to protect Alaska from Japanese invasion. With Canadian assistance, they bulldozed through the wilderness and extended Highway 97 to the Yukon and then on to Alaska. The road was called the Alaska Military Highway at first, then the Alaska-Canada Highway, which was shortened to Alcan before it settled on its present moniker, the Alaska Highway.

Construction began in March 1942 at Dawson Creek, where a railway line and a rough road known as Highway 97 met, and was completed in an amazing eight months. The route followed a line of small airfields between Edmonton and Fairbanks, including, where possible, existing winter roads, old trails and rivers.

Road conditions along the Alcan were nothing short of terrible, with 90-degree turns and 25 percent grades. Gradually the road was improved and today it is even paved. Highway 97 and the Alaska Highway are one and the same from Dawson Creek to the Yukon border, where 97 officially becomes Yukon Highway 1.

In exchange for the right-of-way through British Columbia and the Yukon, the United States paid for construction and turned over the Canadian portion of the highway to the Canadian government in April 1946. The highway officially opened to the public in 1948.

The Alaska Highway runs 2,288 kilometres (1,422 miles) to Delta Junction, Alaska. A 150-kilometre (98-mile) extension from Delta Junction to Fairbanks is officially called the Richardson Highway. ◆

signs that still proclaim its presence.

Dawson Creek's agricultural heritage is apparent from the fields of yellow canola plants that brighten the summer landscape. Canola is a source of cooking oil and is used to make margarine. The leguminous plants produce small, pea-like seed pods that are crushed to obtain the oil. Each seed is

>>> Canola brightens the landscape.

40 percent oil. About 90 percent of British Columbia's production of canola is grown in the Peace. The region takes its name from the Peace River, which you will cross as you go north and which connects this part of B.C. with northeastern Alberta.

Dawson Creek didn't really blossom until hordes of American soldiers camped here during the building of the Alaska Highway. In March 1942, when the first wave of workers arrived, Dawson Creek was a town of 500 people. It still evokes the feeling that you are on the cusp of the frontier, although the area is quite settled and developed. There just seems to be a randomness to the style and placement of buildings, as if things were done quickly with little or no planning. The local people we met were charming, hospitable and extremely proud of their city. They would not dream of living elsewhere, a common attitude among long-time northern residents. Some visitors from the south may harbour such thoughts as "why would anyone want to live in this godforsaken land?" yet there is an intangible pleasure in the serenity, the closeness of nature, the spirit of camaraderie and the nonconformity of not following the hordes to southern cities. Northerners wouldn't have it any other way.

Dawson Creek gets its name from the same source as Dawson City in the Yukon and neither have anything to do with the *Dawson's Creek* TV show. George Mercer Dawson was a geologist, surveyor and explorer who, despite his small stature and deformed back, charted much of the western wilderness.

Attractions
Northern Alberta Railways Park
• Alaska Avenue and Highway 97 N.

This big, green space with the brown grain elevator and old train encompasses several attractions:

> **Dawson Creek Art Gallery:** Housed in a renovated grain elevator annex that uses a system of ramps for displays. Of particular note is a display of photographs of the construction of the Alaska Highway.

> **Mile Zero cairn:** The sign and cairn mark the "true" starting point of the Alaska Highway.

<<< A grain elevator has become an art gallery.

> **Station Museum:** As its name and location suggest, the museum occupies the original train station that was built in 1931. Alaska Highway memorabilia and a video about the building of the road prepare visitors for the northern journey ahead. Lots of railway lore and exhibits will appeal to train watchers.

> **Visitor info centre**

> **Farmers' market:** Saturday mornings, May to October. Visitors are often surprised by the variety of produce that can be grown this far north.

Mile 0 Park

• adjacent to Highway 97

This interesting park is similar to the railway park in that it also contains several attractions:

> **Gardens North:** Several small gardens demonstrate that, even this far north, a profusion of colour can be coaxed from the earth.

> **Rotary Lake:** This is Dawson Creek's swimming hole. The season is short, so jump in while you have the chance.

> **Walter Wright Pioneer Village:** Dawson Creek's history is fairly recent in the scheme of things, so this transported village, with a main street and wooden sidewalks, represents the era from 1920 to 1940. Old cars are parked on the village street.

> **Real McCoy Carriage Service:** A wagon pulled by two stout horses tours the town, accompanied by lively commentary and historic anecdotes by a local narrator.

>>> Pioneer Village recreates recent history.

Mile Zero post

• one block from the tourist info centre, downtown

The downtown mileage post is yet another celebration of the start of the Alaska Highway. Motorcyclists and other travellers like to be photographed here.

<<< Posing for photos is a tradition at the Mile 0 Post.

Events
Dandelion Daze Festival
- Northern Alberta Railways Park
- first weekend of June

A kids' parade in which children dress as their favourite flower, insect, weed (especially dandelion), tree or bird is the highlight. Adults are encouraged to wear pioneer or ethnic costumes and everyone makes dandelion chains. After the parade there is a dandelion chain and count event where the chains are linked and measured and the total number of dandelions is recorded.

Mile Zero Cruisers' Car Show
- downtown
- second weekend of July

The downtown core is closed for this gathering of classic, antique and other nostalgic vehicles.

Peace Country Bluegrass Festival
- Mile 0 Park
- third weekend of July

A full weekend of music takes place at the Walter Wright Pioneer Park, in Mile 0 Park.

Fall Fair Exhibition and Pro Rodeo
- fairgrounds on 116 Avenue
- five days including the second weekend of August
- 250-782-8911

Events include chuckwagon races, an agricultural fair, midway, fireworks, junior rodeo, country music and parade. This is Dawson Creek's biggest annual event. There is also a spring rodeo on the first weekend in June.

Tourist Info
- 900 Alaska Avenue
- 250-782-9595
- www.tourismdawsoncreek.com

On the Road to Fort St. John

In place of the wilderness that you might anticipate, the most northerly agricultural region in Canada continues as you leave Dawson Creek. Productive farms line both sides of the highway. The frost-free growing period here runs, at best, from the beginning of June to the end of August. That's not much time to ripen tomatoes and peaches, but it's long enough to grow grain and feed crops. This is the biggest agricultural area in B.C. with close to a million hectares (2.5 million acres) under production.

Halfway between Dawson Creek and Fort St. John look for a small sign at 220 Road that marks the Old Alaska Highway. Go right and then left at the next junction. This road leads to the only remaining original bridge on the Alaska Highway. Not only that, the Kiskatinaw Bridge is said to be the only curved wooden bridge in Canada. Stop and take a walk across the 162-metre (534-foot) span with a 9-degree curvature. It is delightfully high, and the Kiskatinaw River rushes by in a canyon beneath. Since the load limit is just 25 tons, a new bridge was built west of this one so petroleum trucks and other heavyweights could cross the river. Their previous choice was to ford the river, which they did frequently. On the north side of the bridge a pleasant picnic spot has a sign explaining the bridge's history.

A dozen or so kilometres after the old bridge comes one of the most dramatic vistas on all of 97. As you reach the crest of a hill, suddenly, with Grand Canyon splendour, the Peace River and its steep valley open up ahead and, dare I say, will take your

<<< Curving Kiskatinaw Bridge is original.

breath away. I feel a bit guilty telling you to anticipate the view because I clearly remember the first time I travelled this way, uttering a "Wow!" and leaning forward in my seat to take it all in. Hopefully the visual impact will impress you even if you're expecting it.

As you drive across the Peace River you can ponder the original steel bridge that was built in 1942 and then collapsed in 1957, falling so slowly that no one was injured. A lot of people were inconvenienced when the river crossing had to be made either on a boat or by driving across the train bridge between scheduled trains.

On the north side of the Peace River at Mile 37 of the Alaska Highway sits the industrial town of Taylor, population 1,200. Petroleum industries predominate here, but the friendly folk at the tourist info booth beside the highway will gladly let you know about the local golf course, swimming pool, tennis courts, viewpoints, walking trails and such. The big event of the year is Gold Panning Days, a competition for pros and visitors that has been going on for 35 years. It takes place at Peace Island Park the last weekend in July.

Tourist Info

- 250-789-9015
- www.districtoftaylor.com

 FORT ST. JOHN >>> *population: 17,000*

The little dot on the map serves to prepare you for a sparse frontier settlement, but this part of the province is suprisingly well populated. Big hotels, multiplex cinemas, golf courses and even the ubiquitous big-box stores kick this city up a notch or two from what you might have

>>> Centennial Park sits next to the tourist info stop.

expected. In fact the Fort services towns, villages and First Nations' communities that spread over 25 percent of the land area of British Columbia.

Most of the tourist features are handily grouped together in Centennial Park on 100th Street, next to the tourist info stop. Here you will find a pleasant park with bountiful summer flowers, shaded benches, a skateboard park, water-spray area for kids, historical museum, swimming pool, playground, ice skating arena and big information centre.

The establishment of Rocky Mountain Fort in 1794 gives Fort St. John bragging rights as the oldest non-Native settlement in mainland British Columbia. (Native settlements date back 10,500 years.) The origin of the town's name is uncertain, but popular thought is that the original fort (long gone) was either begun, completed or opened on St. Jean Baptiste Day (June 24). Translated into English, it became Fort St. John.

Attractions
Scenic View

Take 100th Street from the tourist info building, cross 97 and head toward the Peace River. This road ends on a bluff overlooking the winding river, but it seems that this was not quite the end of the road for some automobiles. Look down from various parts of the cliff and you can see the wreckage of cars and trucks of many vintages, an indication that the car toss is an amusement that has spanned many decades. The view puts the Peace into perspective as the river twists through the huge valley, bringing irrigation and power to the land.

Heritage Kiosk Walking Tour
Photos of the way things were are strategically spread throughout town. Start at the info centre and ask for the walking tour map.

Honey Place
• 7.5 kilometres (4.5 miles) south of Fort St. John on the west side of Highway 97
• 250-785-4808

<<< Honey makes money beside 97.

The main attraction of this commercial enterprise is a series of big glass plates among which bees go about their business of making honey. Tubes lead to the outdoors so visitors can watch the bees coming and going. Signs proclaim the biggest glass beehive in the world, and lots of honey products are for sale.

North Peace Museum
• 9323 100th Street
• 250-787-0430

The museum is not difficult to find if you look for an oil derrick pointing to the sky. An oil company donated the 48-metre (136-foot) structure and its base is used as a stage for outdoor performances. The museum is very typical for a smaller town, with a miscellaneous collection that focuses on local growth.

Events
Farmers' Market
• Rec Centre
• 9805 96th Street
• Saturdays from May to December

Fruit, vegetables, baking, preserves, plants, woodworking and other crafts make this an interesting and educational stop. The educational part is talking to the farmers and learning what crops can be raised with such a short growing season.

Rodeo
- Fort St. John Rodeo Grounds
- Bypass Road
- late June or early July weekend

Professional cowboys compete in all the traditional events.

North Peace Fall Fair
- Fairgrounds, Rose Prairie
- late August weekend

The 60-year-old fair is held about 20 minutes from downtown in nearby Rose Prairie. Agriculture-related displays and competitions are the focus: tractor pulls, horse shows, exhibits, judging of plants and animals, plus lots of food and music.

Tourist Info
- 9523 100th Street
- 250-785-3033, 877-785-6037
- www.cityfsj.com

 DETOUR >>> **HUDSON'S HOPE**

Another rare opportunity to take a different route on the return leg of your trip presents itself here. Highway 29 connects Fort St. John to Chetwynd from an intersection just 12 kilometres (7 miles) north of the Fort. This route is slightly shorter than 97, but because of the irregular terrain the drive will take about the same amount of time. The narrow, quiet road immediately gives you a panoramic overview of the fertile Peace River Valley and then descends into the valley to follow the river.

The pretty town of Hudson's Hope, population 1,120, has a full tourist information centre (250-783-9154) and across the road from it, the Hudson's Hope Museum includes several log buildings. In the main building, housed in the original Hudson's Bay trading post, you will find interesting dinosaur fossil displays. Indeed, this is dinosaur country, and the excavations for two nearby dams have uncovered a number of prehistoric bits and pieces that have enabled experts to piece together a picture of life here millions of years ago. The most interesting local character is the hadrosaurus, a duck-billed critter that weighed in at 2,200 kilograms (4,800 pounds).

At the Peace Canyon Dam 10 kilometres (6 miles) south of Hudson's Hope, a three-dimensional mock-up of a hadro dominates the vis-

<<< Tiny Hudson's Hope puts up a big welcome.

itor centre. The centre also features overviews of the dam, dioramas, fossils and historical displays. Self-guided tours explain fossils and history (250-783-9943).

The W.A.C. Bennett Dam, 20 minutes from the village along Canyon Drive, is more tourist-oriented and charges $5 for guided tours. These two sites produce one-third of the power consumed by BC Hydro's customers. The Bennett Dam is earth fill and measures 2 kilometres (1.2 miles) across and 183 metres (550 feet) in height. Its base is 800 metres (2,400 feet) wide, ranking it among the largest of this type of dam in the world. Tours include a film, a visit to the turbines and educational displays (888-333-6667).

<<< The hadrosaurus has not been seen recently.

On the Road to Fort Nelson

The 373-kilometre (230-mile) stretch from Fort St. John to Fort Nelson is one of the least interesting drives on all of 97. A few river crossings, the occasional settlement and some signage are the highlights. Except for the occasional determined farm, agriculture has all but vanished. The trees have become more stunted and while forestry is still a growing concern here, it is less so than farther south. Now oil and natural gas are the major interests and, as we approach Fort Nelson, huge barracks that house the oil workers spread beside the highway. There are 10,000 drilled wells in this region.

 FORT NELSON >>> *population: 4,900*

Spread alongside Highway 97 (sorry, the Alaska Highway) without much planning or pretence, Fort Nelson has obviously grown fast, with an emphasis on function rather than aesthetics. Nevertheless, it is extremely tourist-friendly, offers a few gems and is the last taste of commercial civilization for nearly 1,000 kilometres (621 miles).

When you enter the town from the south, it is hard not to notice the huge industries on either side of the highway. On the left is the largest industrial building of its kind in B.C., a mill that produces plywood and oriented strand board. To the right you can't miss the largest natural-gas processing plant in North America. Duke Energy sends gas from here, via pipeline, to southern B.C. and the United States.

>>> Gas and forests are the resources referred to on this sign.

Named after the British admiral, Horatio Nelson, the town was established more than 200 years ago as a trading post by the Northwest Fur Trading Company. It didn't experience much growth until the Alaska Highway was pushed through. Prior to that it was not much more than a fort that was relocated and rebuilt from time to time. Water routes were the prime method of transportation before the highway was completed.

Attractions

Fort Nelson Heritage Museum

- on 97, north end of town
- 250-774-3536

Museums endure a great deal of competition along 97, as nearly every town sports at least one, and some cities have three or four. At the risk of offending many, I will say that Fort Nelson's museum is the best one north of the US border. In terms of history and variety it may be the best one on all of 97. Although Fort Nelson is more than two centuries old, the museum mostly focuses on the last hundred years. The collection spreads out over an acre or two and, in addition to outside machinery, includes a barn full of old cars dating back as far as 1908, a Hudson's Bay house, a trapper's cabin, a post office and the main museum building. If you love old cars, Marl Brown will talk to you till the cows come home. He'll even crank up the 1909 Brush and you can watch the wood-framed car shudder as its one-cylinder engine pumps out a few horsepower.

<<< The Heritage Museum is Fort Nelson's prime attraction.

Events

Every summer weekday evening except Friday at the Phoenix Theatre at 6:45, a free slide presentation about the town and the Alaska

Highway is offered. Audience size ranges from 60 to 2 (that would be my wife Lian and me).

Tourist Info

Recreation Centre

- on 97, north end of town opposite museum
- 250-774-6400

On the Road to the End of the Road

The seven-hour drive from Fort Nelson to the end of the line at the Yukon border is broken up by an interesting and unexpected array of attractions, both natural and otherwise. Lian and I saw a greater variety of large wildlife north of Fort Nelson than we have seen anywhere else in the world. In addition to the deer, moose and bear that you likely have already seen trucking along the roadside, sightings of caribou, wild sheep and bison will keep driver and passengers alert and entertained. The latter are the biggest surprise, and the hairy 800-kilogram (360-pound) mammals claim the road as their own. Standing up to 2 metres (6 feet) tall and 4 metres (12 feet) in length, the bison have been saved from near extinction. It is the largest land animal on this continent and now numbers 100,000 in Canada.

Another unexpected animal is the Stone mountain sheep, which often congregates at the roadside licking the gravel for traces of the salt that is used to melt snow on the road in winter. Stone sheep have grey or brown coats, while the more common Dall sheep are typically pure white. Stone sheep sport huge curved horns and they are the best of climbers, bounding over cliffs and crags with the adroitness of monkeys in trees.

The third newcomer is the caribou, a big elk-like member of the deer family that in Europe is known as the reindeer. If you have kids who don't show much enthusiasm for the trip to the Yukon, just tell them they are going to see Rudolph and his friends who pull Santa's sleigh. The caribou eke out an existence in some of the world's most difficult and unforgiving terrain. Unique among the deer family, the females and males both sport antlers, and adult caribou weigh between 100 and 270 kilogram (220 to 600 pounds).

Highway 97 leaves Fort Nelson in rather mundane style—relatively straight and flat. However, it quickly springs into life with some truly dazzling scenery. After the initial 80 kilometres (50 miles) it starts twisting and turning as it passes through the tail end of the Rocky Mountain range. This is the most scenic part of the Alaska Highway, what with rivers, lakes and snow-capped peaks. Most of the snow is on the north side of the mountains in summer, so the grandeur of the peaks is even more pronounced for southbound travellers. The road climbs steadily until you reach the highest point on the Alaska Highway at Summit Lake, which is often fog-shrouded, although far from nosebleed altitude at 1,295 metres (4,250 feet).

<<< You can hang your hat at Toad River.

Toad River Lodge, 50 kilometres (31 miles) past Summit Lake, is worth a stop because the café has an incredible collection of baseball caps—more than 6,000 of them. A quarter-century ago one of the proprietors, as a joke, pinned a hat to the ceiling. That started it. The caps probably provide good insulation against the cold, as

row upon row is attached to walls and ceilings. Bring one of your own to add to the collection and write your name and place of origin on its peak.

Muncho Lake, 50 kilometres (32 miles) beyond Toad River, provided a challenge to the Alaska Highway builders: a thin cut had to be pried out of the cliff beside the lake to provide two narrow lanes for traffic. The turquoise water beneath the grey mountains and beside the green forest evokes gasps from those who tend to swoon at the majesty of nature. The water gets its colour from rock ground so fine by ancient glaciers that particles are suspended in it, giving it a greenish tint.

<<< Muncho Lake is a pleasure to behold.

>>> The hot springs at Liard create a microclimate.

Liard Hot Springs, 317 kilometres (197 miles) from Fort Nelson, is a gem not to be missed. Who would have thought that 53°C (128°F) water would flow out of the ground in this desolate, frigid land? More than likely the weather here will be dull and on the cool side, even in July and August, so a soak in the natural mineral waters is a perfect antidote. Liard has two pools. The farthest one, dubbed beta, has water that is just short of hot and is suitable for swimming and splashing. The temperture in the closer alpha pool ranges from skin-peeling scalding to comfortably hot. A warm waterfall in mid-pool gives a nice massage and, at the far end, a small cold waterfall mixes with the hot mineral water.

The hot spring creates a unique microclimate for 250 species of plants, including 14 varieties of orchids. Liard Hot Springs is a provincial park requiring an entry fee to use the facilities. There are camping sites available (800-689-9025, **www.discovercamping.ca**).

The majestic scenery continues north of the hot spring as the road runs beside the Liard River and scampers between mountains. About 25 kilometres (16 miles) past the spring, a sign points right towards Smith Falls. Follow the bumpy gravel road for 2 kilometres (1.2 miles) and you will come to both its end and the falls. Tumbling into a canyon is a double cascade, the roar of which you hear before you see any water. Two sets of old wooden stairs with a total of 170 steps lead to the river. Exactly the same number leads back up.

The next sightseeing stop is Whirlpool Canyon, 40 kilometres (25 miles) distant, and then you enter an area that is slowly recovering from British Columbia's second-biggest forest fire, in 1982. Contact Creek, 145 kilometres (90 miles) from the hot spring, has a sign that explains that two regiments of US soldiers met here as they completed the southern section of the Alaska Highway.

Highway 97 wanders back and forth, crossing the Yukon border

<<< A two-kilometre road ends at Smith Falls.

Sharing the Road with Animals

There are few things as alarming as a 500-kilogram (1,100-pound) moose stepping onto the road as you round a corner at night. If a car hits it, the hooves and antlers can break through the front windshield and lead to the death of both moose and driver.

Two approaches have proven worthwhile in reducing fatalities, and both are in evidence along Highway 97. Clearing a wide swath of vegetation on either side of the highway allows motorists to spot large creatures before they reach the road. And studies show that fences, though expensive, reduce accidents with animals by 80 percent. Unfortunately, cougars, coyotes and bears will dig beneath fences, climb over them or find gaps to squeeze through.

Several methods of animal deterrence are under study. One involves using scents that animals dislike or fear to mark the sides of highways. Another is to place reflectors beside the road that redirect headlights towards animals. Infrared cameras that detect wildlife near a roadway can trigger flashing lights to warn approaching motorists. Cutting back on the use of road salt reduces the number of animals that come to the highways to lick up the residue.

Deer whistles that attach to a car and emit a high-pitched sound audible only to animals have shown inconclusive results. A speeding auto emits all sorts of sounds that humans don't hear, and the deer whistle's shriek may be lost among them.

continued on following page

several times before a sign offers a welcome. This, however, is of little interest to any but those folks who allocate payments for highway maintenance. When 97 makes the final crossing into the Yukon, about a dozen kilometres south of Watson Lake, it officially becomes Yukon #1. However, it is universally known as the Alaska Highway, and the name continues along with the road as it passes through the Yukon and into the state of Alaska.

At the tiny town of Watson Lake, population 1,600, there is but one tourist attraction—the Sign Post Forest, where for 65 years travellers from around the world have been putting up signs pointing (mostly south) to their hometowns. In Watson Lake several roads merge, but none emerges with the number 97 and none can ever be construed as a continuation of 97.

Some Helpful Driving Hints

> All motorists can benefit, when in wild-animal country, from being extra alert and scanning the road ahead from side to side. Animals rarely travel alone. Just as you heave a sigh of relief that you missed the deer that fled across the road, another one is likely to be bounding right behind it. Hooved animals travel in herds.

> Roadside animal-warning signs are not always effective, because animals do not always appear where the signs are placed. Don't stop paying attention when you stop noticing the signs.

> Keep windshields and headlights clean and wipers in good condition.

> Be more aware at dawn and dusk, when animals are most active.

> No matter how cute, cuddly or passive roadside animals may appear, do not feed them and do not get out of the vehicle. These are wild animals; they are very strong and extremely unpredictable. ◆

Where Are We?

Being at the end of the road seems like a good time to take a moment to reflect upon exactly where you are. The 60th line of north latitude divides Yukon and British Columbia. If you followed that line in an easterly direction, you'd cut though the middle of Hudson Bay, the bottom of Greenland and Scandinavia and much of Siberia. If you were able to go as far south as you are north you'd be touching the coast of Antarctica.

The north has very peculiar habits of day and night. In summer there are up to 20 hours of daylight and no hours of true dark. It is possible to go for a walk at 2 a.m. and not need a flashlight. In the depths of winter it never really gets very bright; the sun just peeps over the horizon for a few hours near midday.

>>> North of Fort Nelson, it's not unusual to encounter caribou crossing the highway.

>>> Stone mountain sheep enjoy road-salt residue.

The ignominious end of 97 at the Yukon border is a bit of a letdown for this glorious highway that has taken us so far. There is no link to Weed, California, which proudly proclaimed itself the start of the Alcan Highway, two states and a province away. No cairn commemorates the end of the longest north–south road in North America. No signpost shows the slightest interest in Highway 97, for this is the domain of the Alaska Highway and there is no tolerance for contenders who might steal a clap or two of its thunder.

Although you have reached the end of 97 it need not be the end of a wonderful friendship. The good highway will haunt your memory, and like my wife Lian and me, you will soon have four tires firmly planted on the welcoming asphalt as you head out again and again to explore mountains, crater lakes, hot springs, volcanoes, ghost towns, museums, nostalgic settlements, First Nations heritage, wineries and pioneer villages.

We will likely pass each other on this road and will do so not as two ships passing in the night, but as comrades sharing arcane knowledge about a worthy road known to few.

This is without question a cold land: the thermometer drops below freezing in all but three months of the year, with somewhere around 2.5 metres (91 inches) of annual snowfall. The annual rainfall of 24 centimetres (9.5 inches) is not a lot of precipitation, except that in the summer it doesn't fall in one big deluge, but spatters down drearily day after day.

Northern British Columbia in spring and early summer is a veritable hurricane of biting creatures: the blackflies, no-see-ums and mosquitoes are prolific and persistent pests. Have you heard the story of the two young mosquitoes that entered the tent of two campers? The insects were trying to decide if they should do the bloodletting there, or drag the campers outside. Said one mosquito to the other, "If we drag them outside then we'll just have to share them with the big guys."

The north is also a land full of interesting characters. It takes a unique personality to live in this country and appreciate it. Get to know the people, ask questions, and you'll be surprised by their enthusiasm for their home territory. ◆

Where to Go from Here?

My suggestion, of course, is to make a U-turn and head south so that you can take in more of the greatest vacation road in North America. Other options include continuing to Whitehorse or Dawson City, or even all the way to the Northwest Territories and Inuvik. If that seems overly ambitious, then consider driving to Skagway and using the Alaska ferry system to take the water route south. Or you can follow the Northern Circle Route and take Highways 37 and 16 and meet up with Highway 97 at Prince George. Still another possibility is to continue to Fairbanks, Alaska, and then to Anchorage on the coast and arrange to return, by cruise ship, to a coastal city farther south. ◆

Index

About the Author

Jim Couper is the author of *Discovering the Okanagan* (2004) and is the founder of *Pedal* (Canada's national cycling magazine). He writes for a variety of publications including *Writers' Journal, MotorHome, Trailer Life, RV Gazette* and several newspapers. He has lived in Kelowna, B.C., within 10 kilometres of Highway 97, since moving from the Niagara region of Ontario 10 years ago. He enjoys cycling, tennis, skiing, Scrabble, linguistics and exploring back roads. Jim has edited weekly newspapers in southern Ontario and has owned health food stores, video stores and bookstores. He can be contacted through Heritage House or at okedits@hotmail.com.